BIBLE STUDY

New
Testament
Women

VOLUME 1

FOR

Progressive
Christians

**DONALD
SCHMIDT**

**A SIX SESSION
STUDY GUIDE**

NEW TESTAMENT Women VOL. 1

FOR Progressive Christians

WOOD LAKE

Editor: Michael Schwartzentruber

Proofreader: Dianne Greenslade

Designer: Robert MacDonald

Library and Archives Canada Cataloguing in Publication

Title: New Testament women for progressive Christians / Donald Schmidt.

Names: Schmidt, Donald, 1959– author.

Description: Series statement: Bible study | Includes bibliographical references. | Contents: Vol. 1.

Identifiers: Canadiana (print) 20220215391 | Canadiana (ebook) 20220217033 |

ISBN 9781773435244 (v. 1 : softcover) | ISBN 9781773435251 (v. 1 : HTML)

Subjects: LCSH: Women in the Bible. | LCSH: Bible. New Testament – Criticism, interpretation, etc.

Classification: LCC BS575 .S34 2022 | DDC 220.8/3054 – dc23

ISBN 978-1-77343-524-4

Published by Wood Lake Publishing Inc.

485 Beaver Lake Road, Kelowna, BC Canada V4V 1S5

www.woodlake.com | 250.766.2778

Wood Lake Publishing acknowledges the financial support of the Government of Canada.
Wood Lake also acknowledges the financial support of the Province of British Columbia through the Book Publishing Tax Credit.

Wood Lake Publishing acknowledges that we operate in the unceded territory of the Syilx/Okanagan People, and we work to support reconciliation and challenge the legacies of colonialism. The Syilx/Okanagan territory is a diverse and beautiful landscape of deserts and lakes, alpine forests and endangered grasslands. We honour the ancestral stewardship of the Syilx/Okanagan People.

GOLD

Printed in Canada. Printing 10 9 8 7 6 5 4 3 2 1

CONTENTS

BIBLE STUDY

**New
Testament
Women**
VOLUME 1
FOR
Progressive
Christians

Dedication

To Samantha, Leah, Linda, Lauren, Leilani, Elliet, Annica, and Cora: you are my wonderful granddaughters, and you all have the potential to be powerful women, changing the world. Go for it – and don't hold back!

Thanks

Working with Wood Lake Publishing is a pure delight! Mike Schwartzentruber is more than an editor, but a friend and a guide who takes the words I write and helps them shine. Robert MacDonald, designer, can take what Mike and I produce and make it come to life on the page. Patty Berube and Deb MacDonald, publishers, are good friends and have shown wonderful support to me for many years. Thanks! In a scary and sometimes overwhelming world they seek to produce materials that can help us make sense of it all.

I also express sincere thanks to the various teachers and mentors who have shaped my thinking and have encouraged me to dig behind the face of things such as scripture, and to explore what the Bible itself might really be saying. I'm sure some of them shake their heads at what they unleashed, but I am nonetheless forever grateful.

For group study

This book is designed to be used in group settings, with minimal preparation by leaders. It is intended to encourage open conversation, for which this study guide is simply that – a guide. The questions in each session invite participants to share their thoughts and feelings. The purpose of this study is not to convey certainties, but to invite people to consider these stories, wonder, and then come to their own conclusions.

Here are some suggested ways you might lead this study – but please, make it work for you!

■ Begin by inviting any questions or thoughts folks have had since the previous session. Sometimes a person has had a thought or question lurking in their mind, and it is good to give them a chance to share it.

■ Assuming participants have read the session material in advance of gathering, invite any additional questions or issues that folks are hoping might be addressed. If meeting in person, post a large sheet of paper on the wall and invite people to jot down their questions when they come in. This can provide a sense of anonymity and gives a chance for everyone to look at them as a group and consider them in a manner that makes sense. At the end of the session, allow time to look once again at the list of questions and make sure they have been covered.

■ If meeting virtually (such as via Zoom) people can post their questions through "chat" as they join the session. The facilitator or a member of the group can simply keep the question list and raise them as appropriate.

■ Begin with the questions at the end of each chapter. Conversation will sometimes move you back into the text to explore something in particular; sometimes it will draw in one or more of the questions on the sheet; and sometimes it will lead to other questions – all of which is a great part of the mix!

■ As facilitator, your key job is to keep the conversation on track

B I B L E STUDY

**New
Testament
Women**
VOLUME 1
FOR
Progressive
Christians

and to mediate should there happen to be an entanglement. (This rarely happens.)

■ Perhaps the most important guideline is mutual respect. The process of learning will from time-to-time result in disagreement between participants. But even when there are disagreements, we need to respect the opinions and thoughts of others in the group. All opinions are valid, even ones we may not agree with – it's quite okay handled with respect.

■ Similarly, it is good to remind participants that emotions can run high or we may feel more exposed when we are dealing with issues of faith, which suggests we tread gently with one another, especially when we sense that an issue might be particularly close to someone in the group.

■ It is important to remember that none of us are more "right" than the others in the group. This book does not pretend to provide an authoritative voice; rather, in these pages I have sought to bring out a variety of thoughts and opinions that I have encountered over the years, and to put them forward to provoke thought and conversation. You are free to disagree with the book – and with the facilitator – as well as with each other. The key is to do it with respect for one another.

For individual study

The best thing to do is read the study guide with a Bible close at hand. While the biblical stories are included in the guide, you may want to explore what came before or comes after each story.

Mark the study guide with interesting things you learn from other sources, or with questions. Spend time pondering the questions. You might wish to write responses in the margins, but it's far more important simply to let the questions guide your thinking and reflection.

A note on dates and translations

Throughout this book we use the common designations "BCE" (Before the Common Era) and "CE" (Common Era) rather than the archaic BC and AD. The numbers involved in the dates do not change and using BCE and CE is more inclusive of people of other faiths or of no faith.

There are many good biblical translations of the Bible and in general I encourage you to use the one you like the best. A few comments about some translations:

■ *The King James Version* is full of lovely English poetry, but is not a very good translation. The manuscripts used for the translation have in recent centuries been supplanted by hundreds of other older and far more accurate ones. Additionally, because none of us speak 17th-century English, it can take time to mentally translate the King James English into modern English. It is not helpful for study.

■ *New Revised Standard Version* Done by a group of scholars in the latter part of the 20th century, this translation has generally been held up as being incredibly accurate due to the diligence of a vast editorial team. On the downside, in order to keep it textually close to the original, readability sometimes suffers and it can feel a bit stiff and stilted to some ears. It was also translated at a fairly high reading level.

■ The *Common English Bible* is one of my favourite translations. I find it very accurate, up-to-date, and highly readable.

■ *The Voice* can be especially helpful for those who may not have a lot of biblical background and who struggle sometimes to understand what certain biblical passages mean. The translators (slightly conservative) have occasionally added text. Whenever they do so, the additional text appears in *italics* so you can tell at a glance where the additions are. These additions help flesh out the text and can provide very helpful context, especially given that we are dealing with stories that are thousands of years old and come from a culture and religious milieu very different from our own.

■ *The Message*, a paraphrase by Eugene Peterson with the assistance of several other modern scholars, is arguably one of the most popular versions of the Bible in English. Peterson worked from the original-language texts (Hebrew and Greek). At times Peterson uses more words than other versions to convey not just the literal sense of the biblical message, but the emotional sense. It is amongst the most readable of all Bible versions.

There is no such thing as unbiased history. Over the years, many people have argued otherwise, but they are mistaken. No matter how objective we try to be, we cannot present any story without inserting our own thoughts, reflections, and biases into it.

Imagine this scenario: four people, one after the other, come running into a room.

"A child was just hit by a car!" one of them yells.

Someone else runs in and says, "My friend Kim was driving down the road and had an accident!"

Someone else runs in and says, "Wow – someone just crashed their brand-new car. I think it's totalled!"

A fourth person comes in and says, "Good heavens – there's been *another* accident at that corner."

The stories are all very different. Does that mean that some of them are mistaken? Not necessarily. What it means most of all is that people notice different things, and the things they notice fit with their understanding of the world. More importantly, these are the things that get presented. Sometimes people add things that are clearly meant to lead us one way or another, and we may not even notice. The first person in the example above might have added, "Kid probably didn't look where they were going." The last one might have added, "I told you they need a traffic light there!"

The speakers in each case might not think they are giving a biased story; they are simply reporting what they felt was important. And they want to make sure we understand it the same way. Moreover, the bias of one version over the other is compounded when we identify with one version of the story more than the others (creating a bias of our own), and then declare it "definitive" and put down the others because *they* are "biased."

Everything I've just said about bias is true of the stories and letters in the New Testament, and in the Bible as a whole. Throughout the New Testament, we are dealing with multiple authors, each with their own biases. For example, we have four gospels (Matthew, Mark, Luke, and John) and each of the gospel writers had key points they wished to make. Each gospel has its own particular emphasis and interests. As well, each writer drew on other sources.

11

BIBLE STUDY

New Testament Women
VOLUME 1
FOR
Progressive
Christians

The fact that there has always been a bias against women in Christianity since its earliest days and in the subsequent historical treatments and interpretations of the biblical texts is not exactly news. It shows up in both obvious and subtle ways.

One of the things that is clearly observable both in history and today is that women have been denigrated and put down. They have been censored, they have been shoved aside, and they have been ignored. People have been told not to pay them much attention. As well, the stories in the Bible about women are often shorter, less detailed, and therefore can appear as less important than those about men.

As serious students of the Bible, we can take this as a challenge, as an invitation to dig around the stories to find what the authors may have originally meant to communicate and what the stories can mean for us today. This means we will sometimes need to flesh out the stories of women because we are given so few details. I am hardly the first to suggest this technique, and many of us do this (often unconsciously) as we read and study the Bible. Think of the Nativity stories we hear. When the story of the birth of Jesus is told, people usually insert animals. But there weren't any animals present at the birth of Jesus – at least not in the biblical stories contained in the New Testament – other than the flocks of sheep in the fields that the shepherds were watching. Likewise, having seen countless Christmas cards and pageants, most people are eager to picture a donkey and a cow (and sometimes a handful of chickens) in the place where Jesus was born.

To be clear, there isn't necessarily anything wrong with doing this – in fact, it may be accurate, although we do not know. However, we are also convinced – having been told for centuries – that Mary and Joseph were alone throughout the birth of Jesus. As a result, the suggestion that a midwife or another woman might have helped Mary give birth is often met with dirty looks. To be fair, we don't know that Mary had help from a midwife or other woman

BIBLE STUDY

**New
Testament
Women**
VOLUME 1
FOR
Progressive
Christians

any more than we know there was a cow or a donkey present, but it's worth noting the difference in attitudes. People sometimes bristle at the thought of other women being present but are perfectly content with the addition of cows and donkeys.

In other words, we add things to stories all the time. Unfortunately, we can also get very upset when others add something new to a story or tell a story in a way that differs from how we have heard or told it before.

The bias against women also shows up in more subtle ways. There will always be challenges when it comes to translations because the Bible was written several thousand years ago in three languages: Hebrew, Aramaic, and Greek. In this study, we are dealing with the New Testament, which was written in Greek, about people who spoke Aramaic, who came from a Hebrew tradition – all of which means that when we study the New Testament we are going to bump into language and translations issues.

Let's look at an example. The Greek word *diakonia* and its various forms tend to be translated in two distinct ways. When used in reference to a man, *diakonia* tends to be translated as "deacon," which became a well-established and respected role in the church. However, when the very same word is used in reference to a woman it is usually translated as "one who serves." On the surface, both renderings are legitimate and acceptable – except that over the years the word "deacon" has taken on aspects of "minister," whereas the phrase "one who serves" hasn't. Instead, women have traditionally been told that their role is to serve men, to stay in the kitchen. To translate *diakonia* as "one who serves" only when it is used in reference to women thus perpetuates the notion that women should remain in or be confined to these cultural roles. We have to look, therefore, behind the translations to see what the writers might originally have intended. We also need to ask why distinctions and differences were added to the English text when they were not present in the original. What biases or messages were the translators, both ancient and contemporary, imparting? Do these messages really belong?

Sometimes biases against women can crop up when translators fail to update the English they use. English has changed. Yet many people cling to the phraseology of the *King James Version* – a fine example of English poetry, to be sure – and hold it as the standard against which all other translations should be measured. But our use and understanding of particular words and phrases has evolved since the 1600s, when the translation was done. Nobody speaks or writes like Shakespeare anymore. Our ears simply aren't attuned to that style of English and the meaning of many words has changed. For example, at one time the words "men" and "brothers" were generally understood to include women when used in reference to large groups of people or a society. Today when people hear the words "men" or "brothers," they are more likely to think of an exclusively male group. Thus, when the New Testament clearly refers to a mixed-gender group, the only way we can honestly translate the Greek words is with English words that are inclusive: *humans, humanity, people, folk, brothers and sisters,* and similar words. This is not a case of "changing the Bible" but of being more honest with it.

Of course, I can't talk about biases without addressing the elephant in the room, or on the page, as the case may be. I am a man. I am a man writing a book about women and obviously I'm going to approach this differently than a woman might. But my goal has been to try to present the stories of women in the New Testament – as well as the sexism that has scarred the Christian church and biblical interpretation for centuries – as accurately as possible, and to invite you to notice, to explore, and to celebrate the role of women in the New Testament, as I firmly believe the original New Testament authors intended us to do. I have tried to lift up stories of women whose lives have helped to shape and form my own life and my own faith journey.

Unfortunately, to keep this study to a manageable number of sessions, I have had to make choices about which stories to include in this guide – there are too many for one study. That said, a second study of the stories of women in the New Testament is already in the works. Stay tuned!

Given everything I've written to this point, it is perhaps helpful to remember that we must always read the Bible – and other books – with a few grains of salt. We could look at it and say, "Gee, with all the translation issues and biases, what's the point?" Or we could look at it and say, "You know, despite all its flaws, it has a great deal to tell us."

I prefer that second view. I delight always in exploring the Bible – despite its quirks and variances – and in finding there powerful stories that guide me each day.

Obscure Women

Outside of Ephesus, in modern-day Turkey, an intriguing discovery was made in 1906. It was a cave, and inside was found a painting of a man and a woman. There were two especially significant things about the painting. The first was the identity of the pair; they were Paul and Thecla, a woman of the ancient church and probable travelling companion of St. Paul, at least for part of his ministry. The other significant thing was that Thecla's eyes had been scratched out, and her hand – raised in the traditional stance to suggest one was speaking with authority – had been smudged out.

It is a telling image on a number of fronts, not least of which is the desire of some early vandal to attempt to remove the woman's ability to see or speak. While we can, of course, cannot know the motivation behind the act, it smacks of early Christian sexism and a desire to silence women who dared to claim the authority to speak to others, especially to men. The fact that it was Thecla in the painting might suggest more specific motivations, but we'll come back to that in a bit.

However, as we begin, let's recognize from the outset that from the very beginning of Christianity there has been a concerted effort on the part of men to silence women, to obliterate them, to remove their ability to speak or to act with any kind of authority. Men are generally not comfortable with women who dare to exert individual identity. Now, I can hear lots of people – both men and women – rushing to disagree with me, and yes, there are lots of exceptions. History, however, shows us time and again that women have been relegated to second fiddle or worse. I'll leave it to other scholars to debate why this has happened, and even to what extent. For the purposes of this book, it is simply important to notice from the outset that we have to look diligently for, and at, the stories of women in the New Testament, because the stories of

> A woman's voice is prohibited because it is sexually provocative.
> – *Talmud,* Berachot 24a

BIBLE STUDY

**New
Testament
Women**
VOLUME 1
FOR
Progressive
Christians

women tended to get abbreviated or left out by male writers who simply didn't think women mattered as much as men. Names might have been left out for similar reasons. For some, the mere presence of women in certain stories came under fire, because to leave women in and as present as they appear to have been during the ministry of Jesus was to challenge the status quo.

It's more than just a little ironic that such a thing could happen, because we can clearly see the presence of women at the centre of the community and that they were a key part of the preaching, teaching, and everyday practice of Jesus. The stories we find in the New Testament show us that women mattered just as much as men mattered. It was, rather, subsequent writers, editors, translators, and church leaders who have sought, over the past 2,000 years, to minimize their presence and influence, to discredit it, and to elevate men far above any kind of status they would have experienced in the life explored in the gospels.

Thecla

Before diving into actual biblical stories, let's look for a moment at Thecla. She may or may not appear in the Bible and is certainly not there by name. Her presence may be slight, or major; we can never know, but her story is worth exploring as an introduction to and an example of what has happened to women's stories and presence over the centuries.

Thecla appears in a late second-century text known as the *Acts of Paul and Thecla*. The title alone is interesting, as she is placed squarely with an apostle of great renown. She is portrayed as someone from the upper classes, which means she would probably have been literate, since there was a close link between literacy and class in the ancient world. According to the text, she chose a life of celibacy after hearing Paul speak and was in fact his travelling companion. While that may sound odd, or even wrong, consider the following.

■ It was common for men and women to travel together, and this certainly makes sense in early Christianity because the gospel was about inclusion. What better way to show this than by having men and women go out and proclaim the gospel together?

■ Paul writes to the Corinthians, "Don't we have the right to travel with a wife who believes like the rest of the apostles, the Lord's brothers, and Cephas [Peter]?" (1 Corinthians 9:5).

■ When there is a disagreement between two women in the Philippian church (Philippians 2) Paul asks his "loyal friend" to intervene. It would have been common for a woman to intervene between two other women; the choice of "loyal friend" was a common term for a companion in travel and work.

■ In Acts 16:13, Paul, along with the narrator of Acts, sits down to talk with some women gathered for prayer at the riverside. Had it been only two men who appeared, the women would undoubtedly *not* have spoken to them but would have turned away. But a man and a woman? They could talk to a group of women without difficulty.

This last point is an interesting one, because it suggests that the author of Acts might have been a woman. And this is precisely where Thecla comes to the forefront. Is she the author of the two-volume work Luke-Acts?

Bear in mind that neither the gospel nor Acts ever tells us the name of the author; it is only tradition that assigned authorship to someone named Luke, who was another of Paul's travelling companions. While tradition has some things to recommend it, let us quickly remember that "tradition" told us the world was flat and that the sun revolved around the earth. In other words, traditions are valuable, but they can often be proven to be inaccurate.

It would be difficult to miss the presence of women in the third gospel; indeed, there are more female characters in Luke-Acts than in the other gospels combined. The third gospel also speaks to a number of issues that are of primary interest to women – things such as menstruation and pregnancy. Would a man really have written about such things 2,000 years ago?

Women play key roles in both Luke and Acts: the story of the birth of Jesus focuses almost exclusively on the women; it is women who first proclaim that Christ is risen (and the men think they're

BIBLE STUDY

**New
Testament
Women**
VOLUME 1
FOR
Progressive
Christians

crazy); a woman is presented as an image of God in the parable of the lost coin (Luke 15:8–10). There are also several women *named* in Acts – more than one might find in a lot of other contemporary writings.

It is worth noting that some scholars – notably Jane Schaberg in the *Women's Bible Commentary* – do not like the third gospel and have written copiously about how the stories that include women do so in a secondary fashion.[1] On the other hand, there are scholars – both men and women – who have found astonishing inclusion throughout both volumes.

Does all this prove anything about the authorship of Luke-Acts? Of course not. However, it does not *dis*prove anything, either. There is nothing in Luke-Acts to suggest they were written by a man any more than by a woman, and this is key. We make assumptions about the text and over time we build on those assumptions. They are fed and nurtured by centuries of church tradition that only has room for such things as male authorship and superiority. But there is no evidentiary support for that. In addition, we cannot read the gospels without recognizing that Jesus went to great lengths to include women as fully as possible in the life of the community. Is it not then plausible that a woman might have dared write down the stories of Jesus?

Junia

Junia is an interesting person about whom we again know almost nothing. She appears only once in the Bible, in Romans 16. Paul offers a rather lengthy ending to this letter spending much of chapter 16 listing various friends and colleagues. Roughly one-third of the people Paul greets are women, and of the 12 members Paul lists as contributing the most, more than half are women. This is significant in and of itself. Paul appears to appreciate the presence of women in the ministry of the early church.

And then there's verse 7: "Greet Andronicus and Junia, my relatives [*or* compatriots] who were in prison with me; they are prominent among the apostles, and they were in Christ before I was." A few of the most ancient manuscripts give the name as

BIBLE STUDY

New Testament Women
VOLUME 1
FOR
Progressive
Christians

"Julia" but in either case it is a feminine name. The person being referred to here as a "prominent apostle" is a woman. Are we surprised? We probably should not be – the first apostle of the risen Christ, according to John 20:17 was a woman, Mary Magdalene.

The theologians of the early church assumed Junia to be a female name and thus a female apostle. It is only somewhere around the late 12th or early 13th century that her name began to be listed as Junias (a male name) and her gender was argued as being masculine. Why?

It appears that the earliest church had no problem with Junia being one of two prominent apostles, and yet obviously her gender became a sufficient problem by the 13th century that she underwent a figurative gender reassignment and was christened anew as male.

Her story is important because she illustrates the lengths to which the church has sometimes gone to emphasize the role of men and downplay the role of women. One can only assume that a motivator behind this is fear – fear that noting women as key members of the early Christian community might give them lofty ideals, and that this in turn could be to the detriment of men.

The sisters of Jesus

Even more obscure than Junia are some women who are never named in the New Testament although they are listed on two occasions in Mark's gospel, one of which has a parallel in Matthew. The mere mention that Jesus had sisters has raised more than just eyebrows but a major controversy that can seemingly pit whole volumes of theology against each other.

The box on the next page shows all three references along with a few other verses to provide context.

It's not much to go on, but the reference is there. Jesus had brothers (James, Joseph, Simon, and Judas) and he had sisters. The fact that they are not named neither negates nor diminishes their existence.

Interestingly, "sisters" is lacking in some of the ancient manuscripts of Mark 3:32 and is not present in the parallels in Matthew

> How great the wisdom of this woman [Junia] must have been that she was even deemed worthy of the title apostle.
> – St. John Chrysostom

BIBLE STUDY

**New
Testament
Women**
VOLUME 1
FOR
Progressive
Christians

12:47 and Luke 8:19–20. Yet one has to wonder why: why would someone like Mark have added it? Doesn't it make much more sense that someone would *remove* such a reference?

For some people, the big "issue" at stake in regards to Jesus having siblings – male or female – is that it is an affront to the much later tradition of Mary's *perpetual* virginity. While I understand that this is a hallowed belief in some traditions, I struggle to give it credence and it is not a subject for this study.

So why are these references to Jesus' siblings present at all? The story in its various forms might not have been preserved were it not for the fact that it sets up a tidy teachable moment in which the gospel writers can share Jesus' new understanding of family. Family is larger and broader than mere biology and legal connection, according to Jesus; family is about caring for those close to you and for those who may be more distant neighbours. Doing acts of justice that enhance the lives of other people makes you a member of my family, Jesus says. Having the same biological par-

Mark 3:31–33
[31]Then [Jesus'] mother and his brothers came; and standing outside, they sent to him and called him. [32]A crowd was sitting around him; and they said to him, "Your mother and your brothers and sisters are outside, asking for you." [33]And he replied, "Who are my mother and my brothers?"

Mark 6:2–3
[2]On the sabbath he began to teach in the synagogue, and many who heard him were astounded. They said, "Where did this man get all this? What is this wisdom that has been given to him? What deeds of power are being done by his hands! [3]Is not this the carpenter, the son of Mary and brother of James and Joses and Judas and Simon, and are not his sisters here with us?" And they took offense at him.

Matthew 13:55–56
[55]Is not this the carpenter's son? Is not his mother called Mary? And are not his brothers James and Joseph and Simon and Judas? [56]And are not all his sisters with us? Where then did this man get all this?

ents does not count, at least not by itself. This is not a rejection of biological or legal family, but an enhancement of it.

The widow with the coins

The last "obscure" woman we'll look at in this session isn't actually obscure in that her story is well-known. Yet we know virtually nothing about her – and her story tends to get swept up in sermons about stewardship that don't mention much else. Here's the story.

> ### Mark 12:41-44
> [41] [Jesus] sat down opposite the treasury, and watched the crowd putting money into the treasury. Many rich people put in large sums. [42] A poor widow came and put in two small coppers, which are worth a penny. [43] Then he called his disciples and said to them, "Truly I tell you, this poor widow has put in more than all those who are contributing to the treasury. [44] For all of them have contributed out of their abundance; but she out of her poverty has put in everything she had, all she had to live on."

Luke offers basically the same story, although he omits the opening line that, in Mark, suggests Jesus has sat down specifically to observe the people giving money. We should also note at the outset that there is some controversy over the purpose of the temple treasury. While it had at times been used as a storehouse for gold and other "treasures" and was basically a depository for wealth, at other times it was a storehouse for grain and other foodstuffs to feed the Levites (who tended to the temple) and in fact the surplus was used to feed the poor. But such quibbling can distract us from the point of the story.

Interpretations of the story run the gamut, from people who see this as advice to give all we can, to a quiet condemnation of giving to the temple. Some see the story as a swipe against the rich

BIBLE STUDY

**New
Testament
Women**
VOLUME 1
FOR
Progressive
Christians

for not giving enough more than as a lifting up of the widow for giving all her wealth. Some have even chided – or boldly condemned – Jesus here for not advising the woman to keep her money. Regarding that economic discussion, it is worth noting that Jesus does not in fact praise the woman for her giving.

All of that, however, misses what is most interesting in terms of this study. What is striking is that Jesus notices her at all.

The word "widow connotes one who is silent, one unable to speak" according to the *Social-Science Commentary on the Synoptic Gospels.*[2] Widows went unnoticed, at best, and often were actively ignored. You did not speak to a widow; you did not deal with her other than the bare minimum; you did not support her in any way; she was treated as though she was dead.

Yet Jesus notices her.

In the midst of a great crowd of people giving to the treasury, *she* is the one who stands out, at least for Jesus. He notices an "unnoticeable" person. When everyone else might be noticing the wealthy, commenting on their clothing, marking how elegantly they walk, how much they seem to be giving – and in fact might even be noting the tiny gift of the widow – Jesus notices something different. He sees a person.

This is a bold challenge to a longstanding tradition wherein women who did not "fit" the moulds of normal society had to be ostracized, pushed aside, ignored. We do the same thing today, finding people whom we do not like for a variety of reasons and using various techniques to essentially discard them. Jesus challenges us, in this short story, to act otherwise – to see people for their inherent worth and value. The fact that he points to someone at the bottom of the social heap of his day is especially powerful. That she is a woman is a stinging challenge to those who quickly want to write off women today, using words like pushy, brassy, cheap, wanton, gold-digger, and the like to categorize and swiftly denigrate women. Jesus notices a nobody, and notes that she is in fact a somebody. This is not to be missed.

• • •

All the stories in this session invite us to look a little deeper than the snippets of information about the women than the stories themselves might provide us. They invite us to look at who the women might really be, rather than to simply write them off because we do not have enough information to get to know them. That may have been the intention of the (male) writers who wanted us to ignore the women and focus on the "real" people, who they saw as being far more important.

BIBLE STUDY

New Testament Women
VOLUME 1
FOR
Progressive
Christians

Questions

■ Tradition tells us the place of women in the early church, but scripture often tells a different story. How do you reconcile the two?

■ Paul is often painted as putting women down. However, passages such as Romans 16 suggest otherwise. What do you make of this?

■ Do your thoughts about Paul change knowing that he may have travelled with a female companion? How and why? Or why not?

■ How do you respond to the thought of a woman writing one of the gospels?

■ When you hear the word "disciple," does the possibility of a woman come to mind, or do you primarily associate the word with men?

■ What is your first reaction to hearing that Jesus had siblings? To what extent does that challenge your understanding of Jesus' family or of Mary?

■ In ancient times people looked down upon widows. Who are women in your community who might be treated the same way? Why do you think that is?

■ What might Mark and Matthew be trying to tell us by having Jesus notice a "silenced person" or a "non-person," such as the widow with the coins?

■ How have you heard the story of the "widow's mite" interpreted? With what kinds of feelings has that left you?

■ How might you have felt if you were the woman in this story?

BIBLE STUDY

**New
Testament
Women**
VOLUME 1
FOR
Progressive
Christians

■ Why do you think we have been so quick to dismiss women throughout history?

■ What threat might women have presented to men in society (either in former times, or the present, or both)?

Women at the Birth of Jesus

So much has been written over time regarding the birth of Jesus – both within Christianity and in the secular world – that we are often surprised to learn that it is barely mentioned in the Bible. This should not really be surprising, for the birth of a child in poor families in ancient times was barely noted, and seldom celebrated. The reality that many women and children did not survive childbirth dictated that it was something to be endured; celebration of the birth of the child would happen later. Accordingly, there are very few things about the birth and childhood of Jesus that we can know with any certainty. The stories we do have, however, include several women in key roles.

Matthew tells us very little about Mary, other than that she and Joseph were engaged when she became pregnant, and that they then got married before the child was born – hardly an unusual scenario throughout the ages.

Luke, however, provides more information, including two additional women – Elizabeth and Anna – and implies one more, a midwife. Another woman who would undoubtedly have been present in the overall scene was Mary's mother, known popularly as St. Anne. Rather than get caught up in conversations or arguments about whether or not they existed (if Jesus was a real person, then he *did* have a mother, regardless of whether the stories surrounding his birth are historically accurate), I would prefer to set those questions aside – they're simply not the point of this study. Instead, let's focus on who these women might have been, and what role(s) they may have played.

Elizabeth

The first woman to appear in the third gospel (Luke), Elizabeth, is in fact only mentioned there, in the first chapter, and is never seen

New
Testament
Women
VOLUME 1
FOR
Progressive
Christians

or heard from again. Here is a brief snippet of her story that tells us a great deal.

Luke 1:5-7

In the days of King Herod of Judea, there was a priest named Zechariah, who belonged to the priestly order of Abijah. His wife was a descendant of Aaron, and her name was Elizabeth. [6]Both of them were righteous before God, living blamelessly according to all the commandments and regulations of the Lord. [7]But they had no children, because Elizabeth was barren, and both were getting on in years.

WOMAN'S FAULT

Elizabeth is married to Zechariah who, as a priest, serves God in the temple. They live blamelessly – this must be understood at the outset – yet Elizabeth is barren. Childlessness was generally seen as being the woman's "fault" and was understood to be a punishment from God for some sin she committed. That, however, is not the case here, as both Zechariah *and* Elizabeth are named as "living blamelessly." Thus, we are left with no clue as to their status as a childless couple. We can know, however, that this must have been a huge burden for them to carry, especially for Elizabeth. Because Zechariah is a priest, they do not own land, and thus they do not have a pressing need to have numerous children to work the land as they themselves age. Yet the stigma of being childless was great in most people's eyes.

LEVITIES (PRIESTS)

Elizabeth's role in this story is two-fold: she is the mother of John the baptizer, who sets the stage for Jesus to live out his ministry; and she is the one to prophesy about Mary, affirming that her pregnancy is special and unique.

Zechariah's response to learning that Elizabeth will have a child in old age is disbelief, for which he is "punished" with the inability to speak until the child is born and named. Elizabeth's response, however, is completely different – she accepts the new reality presumably with a great deal of joy. The three-month visit of her "kinswoman" Mary, also pregnant, provides Elizabeth the opportunity to share a great deal about this extraordinary event in her life. Elizabeth boldly declares that Mary is the "mother of my Lord," which is a prophetic act; pretty astonishing stuff for a woman who would have been shunned for being barren for most of her life.

The women of Matthew's genealogy

Before we get to the birth of Jesus in Matthew's gospel, we first have to wade through what many non-Hebrew speakers see as a thick soup of biblical names. It all seems rather ho-hum and some of the names are hard to pronounce, so before their eyes glass over most people ignore the genealogy and go straight to verse 18 to begin their reading in earnest. That's a pity because there is some powerful stuff in the genealogy Matthew presents.

The genealogy of Jesus can be seen as rather classic Matthew – going to historical documentation to support present-day reality. Except he does it in a most curious way; he includes women.

Any quick thought about procreation tells us that a genealogy ought to include the names of both men and women. Yet women are often obscured from historical accounts, and the same is true of ancient genealogies. In biblical times, genealogies were exclusively male, telling us who begat (an old English term for fathering a child) whom. Except for Matthew. Matthew's genealogy includes women – and what a crew they are!

■ **Tamar** (Genesis 38) The law said that if a woman's husband died before producing any children, his brother or other close relative would sleep with her to try to produce a child, who would then be the heir of the deceased man. (This was called Levirate marriage.) This should have happened when Tamar's husband died, but her father-in-law Judah did not allow it. Tamar disguises herself, sleeps with him, steals his identification and becomes pregnant. When Judah learns of this, he wants her killed. However, when she identifies that he is in fact the father, he recognizes that

BIBLE STUDY

**New
Testament
Women**
VOLUME 1
FOR
Progressive
Christians

he had been wrong in the first place, and all is forgiven.

■ **Rahab** (Joshua 2) Rahab is a foreign prostitute who hides some Jewish spies in her house. She lies to the authorities about the men's whereabouts and helps them escape. In return, she and her family are spared when the Israelites enter the land and put everyone else to death.

■ **Ruth** (Book of Ruth) A foreigner of the tribe of Moab, a group generally despised by the Jews, marries a Jewish man who then dies. She returns to Bethlehem with her mother-in-law Naomi, and through a variety of events manages to marry Boaz, a relative of Naomi's who then redeems the two women and restores them to full participation in the life of society.

■ **Bathsheba** (2 Samuel 11) King David sees Bathsheba bathing and insists that she be brought to him for sex; she has no say in the matter. When she learns she is pregnant, she sends word to David. He then calls her husband, Uriah, back from the war where he is fighting in David's army and sends Uriah home to sleep with his wife – presumably so the pregnancy could be attributed to him. Uriah refuses to sleep with her while his colleagues are still sleeping at the front, so David sends him into the area of heaviest battle and Uriah is killed. David then takes Bathsheba into his home and marries her.

These are, of course, fast and furious retellings of a few key events in the lives of these women, provided simply to give a bit of background for those who may not be familiar with them. The stories of these women are covered in detail in the previous study guide, *Women in the Bible for Progressive Christians: Hebrew Scriptures.* These women, and their stories, need our attention because the author of Matthew would not have included them in the genealogy of Jesus without good reason. To put it another way, Matthew would not have stepped this far outside of his tradition unless he wanted to make a major point.

What might that point be? If we look at the specific women who are included, they are all outsiders to some degree. Two (Rahab and Ruth) are foreigners; one (Bathsheba) is the victim of

29

BIBLE STUDY

New Testament Women
VOLUME 1
FOR
Progressive
Christians

rape; and Tamar is forced into prostitution and deceit just to get what the law and society say she deserves. They are brave and risk a great deal just to exert their humanity.

Now, Matthew may have included them to shock us a little, as a way of preparing his readers for the fact that Jesus is going to be born to an unwed mother. His later statement that Mary became pregnant "by the Holy Spirit" (1:18 and 1:20) lacks specifics – there is nothing, for example, to exclude the possibility that she became pregnant through conventional means, and that God was simply behind that (or approved of it after the fact). Thus, Matthew may want us to notice that God has worked with and through women in similar situations in the past. This is what God does; get over it.

On the other hand, Matthew may also have had a larger purpose, perhaps wanting to tell us something about Jesus. It may be that Matthew is trying to say, "Be prepared to have your socks blown off! This Jesus I'm going to tell you about is going to turn the world right-side up. So hang on – this is going to be quite a ride!"

Mary as mother of Jesus

Enter Mary, one of the most famous women of all time. She has been portrayed in such a wide array of forms that it can be difficult to "extract" the biblical person from the baggage that surrounds her. She appears, albeit briefly, a handful of times in the synoptic gospels (Matthew, Mark, and Luke); twice in the gospel of John, although in John she is not named; and she comes back for a final appearance at the beginning of the book of Acts. Some of these stories will be explored in the next session. For now, we focus on the familiar image of Mary the mother of Jesus, the one made famous by countless Christmas cards, pageants, and carols.

For many people, Mary is known not only as the mother of Jesus but also as "the Virgin Mary," as if that is all that matters. Mary's elevation from peasant girl to the Queen of Heaven – which we see in some traditions – is perhaps an extreme example of this. But such theology is not for everyone, including some who grew up with it. In his book *Unexpected News: Reading the Bible with*

BIBLE STUDY

**New
Testament
Women**
VOLUME 1
FOR
Progressive
Christians

Third World Eyes, Robert McAfee Brown describes peasants in Latin America discovering the biblical Mary and recognizing that she has very little in common with the woman they saw portrayed in art – a woman wearing a crown, looking very Caucasian, standing on a crescent moon, and bedecked with jewels.[3] These images, they realized, were a far cry from the woman who sang about God bringing down the mighty and lifting the lowly; about how God has filled the hungry with good food and sent the rich away empty-handed. In Luke 11:27, an anonymous woman shouts out to Jesus, "Blessed is the womb that bore you and the breasts that nursed you!" The bold physicality of this statement is a far cry from the Mary who so often looks serene and beyond human touch in art.

Despite this, the image of Mary as some sort of ethereal "virgin" remains as perhaps the predominant image of her. In great measure this is because of the birth narratives we find in Matthew and Luke. Like the artistic images of Mary as Queen of Heaven, these stories present a tale of mythic proportions. The fact that neither Mark nor John tells us anything about the birth of Jesus is a strong reminder that the stories from Matthew and Luke are primarily works of fiction.

If that's the case, it's natural to ask why Matthew and Luke wanted to include them in the first place. There are a couple of reasons. First, it seems clear that their stories (which differ substantially) were intended to impress pagans who had similar stories, and to carry on the tradition of miraculous conception/birth stories told about great heroic and mythic figures, including those from Egypt and Rome. It is extremely doubtful, therefore, that these stories were ever meant as some kind of entrance exam to Christianity. "Do you believe in the virgin birth? Yes or no." If you answer no, you don't belong; you can't go any further in a spiritual relationship with God and Christ!

The second reason Matthew and Luke might have chosen to include these stories is because, like all myths, they are intended to convey a profound truth. The truth Matthew and Luke wanted to convey is that Jesus was special, and we can see how they did that by looking at the biblical texts.

Of course, when we do that, we encounter the word "virgin" in our English translations. But let's look deeper. The appearance of the word "virgin" in our Bibles results from the fact that Matthew, quoting Isaiah 7:14, mistranslates the Hebrew word *almah* (which means "young woman") as *parthenos,* the Greek word for "virgin," which English translators have pretty much used ever after. It is quite possible, therefore, that the gospel writers simply meant to point out that Mary was a young girl. In fact, many people are shocked to learn how young she would have been. In those days, most women were betrothed at the age of 12, likely because this was around the time that girls matured sufficiently to become pregnant, which was seen as needing to happen within marriage. As a result, girls may have given birth for the first time when they were only 13 or 14 years old.

But if Mary was only a young girl and not a virgin, how did the gospel writers intend to tell us that she was special? Luke 1:35 tells us, "The angel said to her, 'The Holy Spirit will come upon you, and the power of the Most High will overshadow you; therefore the child to be born will be holy and will be called Begotten of God.'" What does that really mean?

The understanding I believe most people carry is that miraculously God somehow had divine relations with Mary, and this resulted in her pregnancy. But let's break down the text a little more. The Spirit of God in ancient Hebrew and in Aramaic thought was always feminine. The Hebrew word translated as Spirit is *ruach* (the "ch" is hard, as in "Bach") and it is a feminine word. The word used to denote the presence of God – *shekinah* in Hebrew – is also feminine. We are thus left with the angel Gabriel essentially saying to Mary, "God's Spirit (female) will come upon you, and the power (*dunamis* in Greek) of the Most High will overshadow you ... "

There's more. The word *dunamis* generally means power, but not merely in the sense of strength and force. It is the word from which we get "dynamite" in English, and it can freely be understood as meaning *inner strength, significance,* and even *miracle.* Is it possible, then, that part of the "miracle" of Jesus' birth is that

> What does God do all day long? God gives birth. From all eternity God lies on a maternity bed giving birth.
> – Meister Eckhart

BIBLE STUDY

New Testament Women
VOLUME 1
FOR
Progressive Christians

> What sort of God would it be, who only pushed from without?
> – Goethe

God imbued ("overshadowed") Mary with the "inner strength" necessary to have a child at such a young age, especially since she got pregnant before she was betrothed or wed? The sense is that somehow a key aspect of God, which is clearly feminine here, will work something quite amazing within Mary, but it may have had as much to do with her unusual openness, courage, fortitude, and inner strength as anything else.

Raymond E. Brown suggests a similar possibility in terms of what the gospel writers might have been trying to say. A leading Roman Catholic theologian of the last century who did major research and writing on the birth and death of Jesus, Brown believed, personally, in the virgin birth. Yet even he conceded that "theoretically, if Mary and Joseph had relations and the child was naturally conceived, Luke might still have looked upon the conception as the work of the Holy Spirit on the grounds that an angel had foretold the conception and that the child was to have a unique role as God's son."[4] This is certainly compatible with Matthew's "she became pregnant by the Holy Spirit" (1:25), which could also just as easily mean "Mary and Joseph had sex and she became pregnant by the Holy Spirit," implying it was a part of the divine plan without having to be something that happened without sex. Think about it. How many new parents today experience their newborn as "a gift from God," or believe that their pregnancy was "meant"?

These are all ways the gospel writers may have tried to communicate through their stories that this pregnancy, and this child Jesus, and this mother and father – let's not forget Joseph's courage as well – were indeed special. Filled with the power of the Spirit of God, they stepped up to the plate to help bring God's dream of "God with us" (Emmanuel) to reality. And all of this without necessarily intending to imply that Mary was a virgin.

This interpretation of the text has real-world implications for so many women today. For too long in our male-dominated culture, the notion of Mary's virginity has served to perpetuate the sexism that a woman is more "pure" or somehow "better" if she does not have sex. But such a notion is not supported by the New

Testament. (For more discussion of these stories, see my earlier study *Birth of Jesus for Progressive Christians*.)

Mary's mother

Mary's mother does not appear in the Bible but turns up in later legends and is featured in the doctrine of the Immaculate Conception, a controversial doctrine of the Roman Catholic church that is probably one of the most misunderstood of popular beliefs.

Mary's mother is traditionally known as Anna or Hannah, and in modern English becomes St. Anne – highly revered in parts of Quebec, among other places. No one cared too much about her, although she was written about in an early book known as the Protoevangelium of James (or the Gospel of James). That changed when Augustine of Hippo (354–430 CE) came up with the doctrine of "original sin," which eventually became the official position of the Roman Church. Augustine did this by inserting original sin and the Fall into the story of the Garden of Eden and Paul's Letter to the Romans.[5] In short, the doctrine suggested that all humans inherently sinful because they are conceived sexually.

What would that mean for Jesus? He was "fathered" by God, but his mother would still have been conceived sexually. To remedy this, it was decided that Mary must also have been conceived without sex (immaculately) so that Jesus would be free from this "curse."

This is the doctrine of the Immaculate Conception – that Mary was conceived non-sexually so that she could avoid passing along original sin to Jesus. It seems a shame to have added such a bizarre burden to Anne, whoever she was in real life, who already had to deal with the public shame of a daughter who was pregnant out of wedlock.

The midwife

This woman seldom – if ever – appears in Christmas cards or dramas. A notable exception was a BBC video called *The Nativity* that was released in 2010, one of the first major dramatic presentations of the story of the birth of Jesus that included someone other

"Virgin Mother" shows the fear and degradation of birthing and female sexuality of the male-dominated church.
– Chung Hyun Kyung, *Struggle to Be the Sun Again*

BIBLE STUDY

**New
Testament
Women**
VOLUME 1
FOR
Progressive
Christians

than Mary and Joseph all alone in the stable. The truth of the matter will, of course, never be known, but it is extremely unlikely that no one noticed Mary and Joseph enter Bethlehem and that any woman who saw an incredibly pregnant young girl would not offer to help her as she went into labour. Therefore, we can safely assume that there was a midwife present at Jesus' birth and was left out of the story because, well, she "didn't matter." It is worth a moment of pause to remember her, and to give thanks for someone who helped bring Jesus into the world.

Anna

> ### Luke 2:36–38
>
> [36]There was also a prophet, Anna the daughter of Phanuel, of the tribe of Asher. She was of a great age, having lived with her husband seven years after her marriage, [37]then as a widow to the age of eighty-four. She never left the temple but worshiped there with fasting and prayer night and day. [38]At that moment she came, and began to praise God and to speak about the child to all who were looking for the redemption of Jerusalem.

The title "prophet" is frequently reserved for men, yet Luke calls Anna a prophet (while at the same time only refers to Simeon as "righteous and devout"). She is a widow, and the third gospel has a penchant for widows, referring to them more than all the other gospels combined. Anna's genealogy is given in verse 36, rather than that of her husband. Those are the positive features about Anna we are told in these few short verses.

Although the author of Luke-Acts does not give her a speaking part in his story, the narrative tells us that she spoke to everyone about Jesus, telling them that this child was going to be the redemption of Israel. Apart from all of that, Anna is an interesting character. Her age is symbolic: 84 years is 7 (the number for perfection) multiplied by 12 (the number of the tribes of Israel). Her given age, then, conveniently hints at Jesus being the culmination of all the hopes and dreams of the nation. Her standing seems slightly higher than that of Simeon, and she belongs in the proud tradition of widows from Judith (a great heroine of Judaism) through the exemplary widows of early Christianity who devoted themselves to ministry. It could even be noted that while early widows were recognized for ministries of hospitality – caring for the sick and feeding the hungry – Anna takes on a ministry of word, the message she proclaimed, and not for acts of tea and sympathy.

Anna is truly a woman prophet who proclaims the importance of Jesus in the designs of history – no small achievement.

All the woman involved in the stories of the birth of Jesus play significant roles. If nothing else, they remind us that woman are not only the ones who birth children, but also are frequently the ones who directly influence their upbringing.

Questions

The questions in this session are based on inviting participants, in turn, to imagine they are the women who were discussed, and wondering about some of their feelings. This may take the conversation in directions you had not anticipated – go with it!

■ Why do you think Matthew has included women in his genealogy, and why these women in particular?

■ How important is the issue of Mary's virginity to you?

■ How do you understand the "power" of God that overshadowed Mary?

■ You are Elizabeth. You're an older woman and have spent most of your life being laughed at and having people discuss (behind your back mostly) whatever you might have done wrong to cause you to be barren. How do you feel about that?

■ You have just learned you will have a child, now that you are old. How do you feel? What hopes do you have? What fears?

BIBLE STUDY

New Testament Women

VOLUME 1

FOR

Progressive Christians

■ What about your husband, Zechariah? You are quite sure he loves you, and yet he has questioned your worth and value, and wondered what he, too, might have done wrong. Now he is unable to speak at a time you most want to talk to him. What might you ask him if he could speak?

■ Your relative Mary comes to visit and you learn she is also pregnant, even though she is young and unmarried. What kinds of things might the two of you discuss during the several months she stays with you?

■ You are Mary, age 13 or 14, pregnant, and unmarried. People throw things at you, call you a slut, and spit at you in the marketplace. How do you respond?

■ You want to help Joseph understand what's going on. How might you do that? How do you think he might react?

■ You are Mary's mother. Your teenage daughter has just told you she is pregnant, and that it is some sort of miraculous thing involving God. What makes you want to believe her? What keeps you from believing her? What feelings do you have about her, and for her?

■ Imagine you are present later in life, as your grandson Jesus is growing up. How do you feel about the things he is teaching, that challenge your faith and life?

■ You are a midwife and you have noticed a very pregnant young girl come into town. There is a young man with her – presumably her husband – but her youth suggests this is her first child. She appears terrified. You offer to help and the young couple welcome you. What do you say to her/them?

■ Some shepherds arrive and tell you about a visit from an angel and about the child's place in history. What do you make of this?

■ You are Anna. You have lived for far too many years as an elderly widow, and now just as your life is drawing to a close you encounter the infant Messiah, the hope of your people. How does that make you feel? What news about him do you want to share with others?

■ Luke says you are a prophet. What do you think of that?

Mary of Nazareth

You'd be forgiven for assuming that Mary of Nazareth disappears from the Bible shortly after the birth of Jesus. To be fair, her appearances later in the gospels are few and far between, but they are significant in several ways and remind us that Mary was more than a mere device to birth Jesus. Mary was in fact quite involved in his life and, after that ended, his ongoing ministry. In this session we will explore four of her appearances in scripture. (The story of Mary and John at the cross and the additional possible appearance on Easter Sunday will be explored in a sequel to this study.)

The following story is offered to us only in the third gospel and seems to be intended to show that Jesus knew early in his life that he was special, and a child of God. The fact that he is 12 in the

Luke 2:41-50

41Now every year [Jesus'] parents went to Jerusalem for the festival of the Passover. 42And when he was twelve years old, they went up as usual for the festival. 43When the festival was ended and they started to return, the boy Jesus stayed behind in Jerusalem, but his parents did not know it. 44Assuming that he was in the group of travelers, they went a day's journey. Then they started to look for him among their relatives and friends. 45When they did not find him, they returned to Jerusalem to search for him. 46After three days they found him in the temple, sitting among the teachers, listening to them and asking them questions. 47And all who heard him were amazed at his understanding and his answers. 48When his parents saw him they were astonished; and his mother said to him, "Child, why have you treated us like this? Look, your father and I have been searching for you in great anxiety." 49He said to them, "Why were you searching for me? Did you not know that I must be in my Father's house?" 50But they did not understand what he said to them.

BIBLE STUDY

**New
Testament
Women**
VOLUME 1
FOR
Progressive
Christians

story could be a symbolic way of Luke saying that Jesus was "perfect" or "complete" – 12 was often used to denote such things. He may also simply have been 12; we cannot know.

Some people are taken aback that Jesus' parents do not notice him missing for a full day, but this is hardly surprising – the entourage that travelled to Jerusalem would have included many from their extended families, as well as other people from their village, and it would not have been unusual for children to travel with others in the group. Youngsters often like to hang out together, away from mom and dad. What is intriguing for our purposes here is to note Mary's response to Jesus when she finally encounters him.

Mary is upset, as we would expect any mother to be. It's that moment when the parent is torn between hugging and strangling their child. "How could you do this to us? We were worried sick. Oh, I'm so glad we found you. Don't ever do that again! Are you okay?"

Jesus responds rather smartly for a 12-year-old: "Didn't you know I would be in my father's house?" We cannot know the mood; it might have been said rather flippantly, or with a gentle sense of "sorry, I didn't think." Once again, the parental response is intriguing in that Mary and Joseph do not understand; presumably Mary would have known that Jesus was special. It is left to us to assume that after this incident things will be different.

How would Mary respond? How would *you* respond?

Mark 3:31–35   *LATER IN LIFE*

³¹Then [Jesus'] mother and his brothers came; and standing outside, they sent to him and called him. ³²A crowd was sitting around him; and they said to him, "Your mother and your brothers and sisters are outside, asking for you." ³³And he replied, "Who are my mother and my brothers?" ³⁴And looking at those who sat around him, he said, "Here are my mother and my brothers! ³⁵Whoever does the will of God is my brother and sister and mother."   *(FAMILY)*

We first looked at this passage in Session 1, where we considered the reality that Jesus had sisters as well as brothers.

The context seems to be that Jesus' teachings have gotten out of hand, at least in the view of his family. They have heard what he is teaching and appear to have come to take him home. At least that's how it seems. However, it's not clear that this is how the crowd, which presumably included the disciples, interpreted their presence.

Mary and Jesus' brothers – and possibly sisters – arrive and send word to Jesus that they have come for him. When Jesus is told that his mother, brothers, and sisters have arrived, he uses it as a teachable moment and explains to the wider group that true family is not defined as those who are related to us biologically, but rather as those who do God's will, as noted in Session 1. Matthew and Luke both relate a similar version of this story although neither of them includes the reference to sisters, possibly because later writers and editors wanted to downplay any potential reference to the ministry of women.

Either way, it is intriguing that Mary and some of Jesus' siblings have come to bring him back – back simply to their home, or back to a more orthodox line of teaching? We can never know. Of course, the story may simply be symbolic, a way the author chooses to recognize that some people felt Jesus needed to be brought back to a more "acceptable" or traditional presentation of the faith. If that's the case, then Jesus' explanation that what matters is doing the will of God would have been intended by the author as a biting rebuttal to forces that still felt that way.

Mark 6:1-3

[Jesus] left that place and came to his hometown, and his disciples followed him. ²On the sabbath he began to teach in the synagogue, and many who heard him were astounded. They said, "Where did this man get all this? What is this wisdom that has been given to him? What deeds of power are being done by his hands! ³Is not this the carpenter, the son of Mary and brother of James and Joses and Judas and Simon, and are not his sisters here with us?" And they took offense at him.

BIBLE STUDY

**New
Testament
Women**
VOLUME 1
FOR
Progressive
Christians

This text exists in various forms and has (presumably) been altered slightly by both Matthew and Luke. One issue here is the word translated as "took offense" in verse 3, which in Greek literally means "stumbled." It doesn't quite make sense, and so translators scramble a bit to figure it out. In *The Message,* Eugene Peterson took a very literal approach: "They tripped over what little they knew about him and fell, sprawling." It kind of works, but the bottom line is that the meaning or intent of the original text is a bit unclear.

The more intriguing piece for our purposes is the beginning of verse 3, where Jesus is described as "son of Mary." Normally, a person's family connection would be defined or stated through the father, and a few of the ancient manuscripts correct the text to read "son of the carpenter and of Mary," which is what Matthew has. Luke goes with "Joseph's son" and omits Mary completely. Yet if we subscribe to the theory often used in translation that a text would be changed to make it *less controversial,* not *more* controversial, and given that Mark is generally considered the earliest gospel, then we are left with the probability that Mark's version is the most accurate

Some scholars have leapt upon the reference to Mary and the omission of Joseph as implying that Joseph had died. As mentioned before, some have used this to argue that Jesus could not have had siblings. However, because this story takes place when Jesus is an adult that argument doesn't hold much water since several siblings could have been born before Joseph died. Furthermore, it's negated by Matthew and Luke.

So this passage raises two principle questions. Why would Mark have wanted to identify Jesus as "son of Mary"? Was it perhaps to recognize how Jesus worked to enhance the role of women in society? Or was it because his father had died, as some scholars argue?

Whatever position you take, the primary point of the passage is to show that some people in Jesus' hometown wanted to discredit him. They appear to be intrigued by his teaching, but immediately begin to poke holes in his pedigree, which was *everything* in biblical times. You were born into a "caste" or "station" or role, which the vast majority of people never rose above. Even to try to rise above it was frowned upon. The question "isn't he Mary's son?" is thus a putdown. He's a nobody. "We know his parent(s) and his siblings, and they're nobody special, so he must be a nobody, too."

Next we turn to a passage from John's gospel that is well-known as a miracle story, but which goes far beyond that. Some traditions see the story of the wedding at Cana primarily as Jesus' affirmation of the tradition of marriage – a stretch, given that many people attend weddings without venturing an opinion on marriage as an institution. Others of a more Puritan bent struggle to affirm a story in which Jesus creates copious amounts of high-quality wine. Still others wonder about the relationship between Jesus and his mother in the story, and about her significance in it.

It helps to remember that "in John's Gospel, virtually every aspect of the Jesus story is symbolic."[6] This does not necessarily

BIBLE STUDY

New Testament Women
VOLUME 1
FOR
Progressive Christians

John 2:1-11

On the third day there was a wedding in Cana of Galilee, and the mother of Jesus was there. [2]Jesus and his disciples had also been invited to the wedding. [3]When the wine gave out, the mother of Jesus said to him, "They have no wine." [4]And Jesus said to her, "Woman, what concern is that to you and to me? My hour has not yet come." [5]His mother said to the servants, "Do whatever he tells you." [6]Now standing there were six stone water jars for the Jewish rites of purification, each holding twenty or thirty gallons. [7]Jesus said to them, "Fill the jars with water." And they filled them up to the brim. [8]He said to them, "Now draw some out, and take it to the chief steward." So they took it. [9]When the steward tasted the water that had become wine, and did not know where it came from (though the servants who had drawn the water knew), the steward called the bridegroom [10]and said to him, "Everyone serves the good wine first, and then the inferior wine after the guests have become drunk. But you have kept the good wine until now." [11]Jesus did this, the first of his signs, in Cana of Galilee, and revealed his glory; and his disciples believed in him.

BIBLE STUDY

New Testament Women
VOLUME 1
FOR
Progressive Christians

mean that the stories are false or made-up, but it clarifies that John will, if necessary, sacrifice the facts in favour of using symbolism to make a point.

This becomes evident at the very beginning; where the wedding happens "on the third day" – a clear reference or allusion to something else that happened on a third day, the resurrection. In other words, "the Wedding at Cana" is a hugely symbolic and important story, right up there with the resurrection story itself. And in case we missed the point in verse 1, John hammers it home again at the end, in verse 11, where we are told that Jesus did this "and revealed his glory."

Another intriguing aspect of the story is that Mary is mentioned first, suggesting that she is the key character. When Mary tells Jesus that they have run out of wine, he responds with an odd phrase: "Woman, what concern is that to you and me? My hour is not yet come" (verse 4). Is he being rude? Is this a kind of "Give me a break, lady. Leave me alone; I'm not ready yet" spoken in anger? Or is it more condescending, as in "How dare you rush me!" or more playful and offered with a wink, to suggest, "Okay, Mother – you know best!"?

My own preference is to read it as playful. It's not that I struggle with Jesus being rude – after all, the next story in John has Jesus make a whip to drive people out of the Temple, so I know he's capable of it. Rather, I prefer to think that Jesus is working *with* Mary here, and not against her.

Either way, Mary is clearly a major player in the story. She – a "mere" woman – offers the potent instruction to the servants to do whatever Jesus tells them. Why would they listen to her, unless they know she is a woman of some standing in her own right? Jesus tells the servants to fill some massive stone jars (holding between 120–180 imperial gallons, or 550–820 litres) with water. It miraculously turns into wine – and high-quality wine at that. Even if there were a couple hundred guests at the wedding, they've already had a fair amount to drink, and now there's at least three or four more litres apiece. Exaggeration? Undoubtedly. But John is not concerned with facts; John wants to tell a good story and to say something about who Jesus is.

We should not miss the fact that Mary is present at the first "big" story in John's gospel. Rather than show her as the one who gives *birth* to Jesus (John doesn't have a birth narrative per se), John wants to show Mary as the one who *births Jesus' ministry*. What better way than at a wedding? It's a perfect setting to demonstrate that the messianic era, signalled by a great messianic banquet, has begun. The wedding brings together the entire village, and relatives from afar, for an unparalleled celebration – the bringing together of two families, and the creation of a new one. Jesus – at Mary's urging and insistence – has made it a banquet beyond anyone's wildest imagination, inviting everyone to know that the reign of God has arrived, and it too is a good and amazing thing, far beyond anyone's wildest dreams.

There is yet another explanation for why John has Jesus say "woman" rather than "mother," and for saying the wedding happened on the third day. Depending on how one counts the days that John presents in chapter 1 of the gospel, this could the seventh day, not the third day. The gospel begins with the potent words "In the beginning ..." all readers throughout history are immediately drawn into the creation stories in Genesis. Some then see Mary's role here as being akin to that of the first "woman," Eve, which is Hebrew for "mother of all nations." As the creation of Eve can be seen as the culmination of God's work in the first creation, so is Mary pivotal now in ushering in the new creation – the restoration of the entire cosmos to full alignment with the divine Creator.[7] We are thus invited to understand the new creation as a great party with an overflowing abundance of wine – a celebration of humanity, of creation, and of a renewed relationship with God. Not bad at all.

BIBLE STUDY

**New
Testament
Women**
VOLUME 1
FOR
Progressive
Christians

Acts 1:13–14 *After Crucifixion*

¹³When they had entered the city, they went to the room upstairs where they were staying, Peter, and John, and James, and Andrew, Philip and Thomas, Bartholomew and Matthew, James son of Alphaeus, and Simon the Zealot, and Judas son [or brother] of James. ¹⁴All these were constantly devoting themselves to prayer, together with certain women, including Mary the mother of Jesus, as well as his brothers.

Mary's last appearance in the New Testament is very slight but significant. It comes at the beginning of Acts, Luke's second volume about the ministry of Jesus. Acts begins right after the death and resurrection of Jesus and so shows us that the life of Jesus continues even after he is no longer physically present. His ministry will grow and spread throughout history.

Coming directly on the heels of Jesus' ascension into heaven, this story establishes the life of the church. The early church – the first community of disciples – is not just a group of 12 men, as too many of us have assumed for far too long – but is a much larger group of people who followed Jesus. A handful of them are named here *including* Mary the mother of Jesus, and his brothers. There are others besides, I hasten to add, both men and women. Mary is the only woman named, but that fact alone is a strong one, for it places her as a significant participant in the life and work of the early church. She did not have a bit part confined to pageants and Christmas cards but has been present throughout the life and ministry of Jesus and continues with it now that he is physically gone.

• • •

Mary is a key figure in the life of Jesus – not just as the one who birthed him, but as much more. It is vitally important, I think, that we grasp this because it helps us realize that women in general were very present in his life and ministry. They are not just the objects of miracles and healings, but play significant roles, whether it is showing up to bring Jesus out of a difficult situation or challenging him to get going with his ministry (how many of us have had our parents do this more than once!) or continuing his life's work after his untimely death. It seems the young girl who sang the Magnificat at the beginning of the Jesus story meant it.

BIBLE STUDY

New Testament Women
VOLUME 1
FOR
Progressive
Christians

Questions   *Special Person*

■ If you were Mary on the journey home from the Temple visit in Jerusalem how would you have felt when you discovered Jesus missing? When he was found in the Temple? When he offered his unusual explanation?

■ Imagine growing up in a large family with Jesus as one of several siblings. What might that have been like?

■ What do you make of the fact that texts dealing with Jesus' siblings – especially his sisters – may have been altered?

■ What does it mean to refer to Jesus as son of Mary (as opposed to son of Joseph)?   *May Have Been Depp=*

■ In the story of the wedding at Cana do you think Jesus is angry with his mother, or apprehensive, or even playful?

■ What happens to the story depending on the understanding of his mood we choose?

■ Former general secretary of the World Communion of Reformed Churches Rev. Chris Ferguson once preached a sermon on John 2:1–11 in which he referred to Mary as the midwife of God in this passage, the one who prodded Jesus to begin his ministry. What does that image mean to you?

■ How do you react to the statement "in John's gospel virtually every aspect of the Jesus story is symbolic"?

■ What might be symbolized by the gargantuan amount of wine Jesus creates in Cana?

■ What might be the significance of naming Mary in the story of the early church gathering in Acts 1?

Women Disciples

Mention the word "disciple" and probably people think of the 12 men named by Jesus in the gospels. There were, of course, a lot more people who followed Jesus, who offered leadership within the Jesus community, and who shared the good news about Jesus far and wide. Some of those people were women.

The female disciples, however, are not often mentioned and, when they are, they are often given only cursory attention. Their ministries, though, while not described in great detail, are powerful. The various stories of Jesus feeding a huge crowd provide a perfect example. These stories appear a total of six times in the gospels – twice in each of Matthew and Mark, and once each in Luke and John. Depending on the story, the number of people present is usually given as 4,000 or 5,000. Matthew, however, describes it a little differently saying, "And those who ate were about five thousand men, besides women and children" (14:21) and "Those who had eaten were four thousand men, besides women and children" (15:38).

What are we to make of this? Why are the women and children not counted? In the society of the day, women and children had no status apart from a significant male – their father, husband, or other male family relation (brother, brother-in-law, uncle, etc.). Yet the fact that their numbers wouldn't have been counted doesn't negate their presence nor its significance. If anything, their presence enhances the story as it suggests that a much larger group was fed.

We should hasten to add that numbers are not really the issue here – which is good, because that size a group would have been quite impossible in those days. Rather, the point the gospel writers wanted to show is that Jesus commanded a huge, unwieldy crowd – more people than could be imagined.

Never once did Jesus scan the room for the best example of holy living and send that person out to tell others about him. He always sent stumblers and sinners. I find that comforting.
Nadia Bolz-Weber, *Accidental Saints: Finding God in All the Wrong People*

The story reminds us that women were usually present in whatever events the ancient stories describe but were rarely considered important enough to be included in the story per se. This shouldn't surprise us; this attitude has existed in most cultures until very recent times. As a case in point, of the 20 statues on Canada's Parliament Hill in Ottawa, Queen Victoria was the only woman represented until 1992 when Queen Elizabeth joined her. The five women who contested and won the Persons Case that determined women to be persons under law were given a statue in 2000, and one woman was depicted along with six men in the War of 1812 monument erected in 2012. In other words, one-fifth of the statues depict women who make up just over half of the population. The United States does not fare much better. A mere nine statues, or 9%, of the 100 statues at the U.S. Capitol Building are women.

When we read the rare mentions of women in the scriptures, therefore, we need to read between the lines to a certain extent; we need to dig a little deeper than the brief mentions they are given to flesh them out as best we can.

It is worth noting that there are different categories of disciples within the New Testament. There are "the twelve," called by Jesus and named on a few occasions. These are all men. Many scholars have pointed out that the fact that there are 12 is intended to link them to the 12 tribes of Israel. Viewed from this perspective, Jesus is creating a "new Israel" or new community of God's people.

Within the 12 there is a smaller group consisting of Peter, James, and John, who Jesus occasionally takes with him on special assignments. There is one woman named as a disciple (Dorcas, or Tabitha, in Acts 3:36) and one named as an apostle (Junia, whose story we explored in Session 1). There are many others who followed, or who were sent out (which is what "apostle" means) even though they are not given that title. We also know that the author of Mark had a not-so-great view of the male disciples, noting that by the time of the crucifixion they had all fled, leaving only the women to stand in support of Jesus. Whatever name or title the

BIBLE STUDY

**New
Testament
Women**
VOLUME 1
FOR
Progressive
Christians

followers of Jesus were given, we know the group contained both men and women.

Peter's mother-in-law

This woman is fascinating for a few reasons, not least of which being that her existence tells us that Peter was married, which is not something we are told or can glean anywhere else. The fact that she is living in Peter's household – with her daughter and son-in-law – also suggests that she is a widow and thus may need Peter (as son-in-law) to validate her existence and give her standing in the community, as already noted,[8] and that she has no son, though we cannot know for sure about this latter possibility.

It's also intriguing that her story – only two or three verses depending on the version – appears in all three synoptic gospels.

> ### Mark 1:29–31
> [29]As soon as they [or he] left the synagogue, they entered the house of Simon and Andrew, with James and John. [30]Now Simon's mother-in-law was in bed with a fever, and they told him about her at once. [31]He came and took her by the hand and lifted her up. Then the fever left her, and she began to serve them.

The context in Mark's gospel is interesting. Jesus was walking along the beach and called Peter and Andrew to follow him, which they do without hesitation. A moment later Jesus noticed James and John fixing their fishing nets and they got up and followed, too. Jesus then went to teach in the synagogue and people were amazed because he taught "with authority, not like the legal experts" (1:22, *Common English Bible)*. Jesus was confronted by a demon, which he cast out, and immediately the word about Jesus spread far and wide. Fresh on the heels of this rather hurried and profound series of events comes the healing of Peter's mother-in-law.

Matthew places the story much later, after considerable teaching, and follows it up with stories about many others who brought sick and injured people to Jesus for healing. Luke's version is closer to Matthew's, although with not quite as much teaching beforehand.

What is profound about the short story is the use of the word for "served" in verse 31. The Greek verb used is *diakoneo* and it literally means "to serve." Greek culture did not value serving others, believing that men were born to rule and not serve. In contrast, Hebrew culture valued service to others as a profound obligation that could earn one honour or at least appreciation. *Diakoneo* had the sense of serving at table and thus taking care of someone's most basic needs. Over time in the early church, the word was used for those who held a specific job – the job of deacon. These people practiced ministries of serving at table (some have suggested that this included presiding at the meal that would evolve into communion). They also took food to those who were hungry, and cared for widows, orphans, and those who were sick. It was a highly revered job and it could be held by both men and women (1 Timothy 3:11). Later tradition assumed that the female term referred to deacons' wives, but there is nothing to suggest that other than theological sexism.

All of this brings us back to the point in the story when Peter's mother-in-law is healed and immediately begins to serve Jesus and the others. This "service" might have involved making them some dinner, perhaps as a way to thank Jesus. But it could also mean that she became a follower of Jesus and thus in this moment began a ministry of service to Jesus and very possibly to others much more broadly.

Mary Magdalene, Susanna, and Joanna

Mary Magdalene appears a number of times in the gospels, including in Luke 8 where she appears alongside Susanna and Joanna. By comparison, Susanna is only mentioned once, in Luke 8; and Joanna is mentioned twice, once in Luke 8 and again as one of the women who goes to the tomb in Luke 24. In both cases the refer-

BIBLE STUDY

**New
Testament
Women**
VOLUME 1
FOR
Progressive
Christians

ences are very slight and almost incidental. Except of course they are not; they provide opportunities to question and to wonder.

Luke 8:1–3

Soon afterwards [Jesus] went on through cities and villages, proclaiming and bringing the good news of the kingdom of God. The twelve were with him, ²as well as some women who had been cured of evil spirits and infirmities: Mary, called Magdalene, from whom seven demons had gone out, ³and Joanna, the wife of Herod's steward Chuza, and Susanna, and many others, who provided for them [or him] out of their resources.

Not much, is it? A brief mention of three women who supported the ministry of Jesus and the other disciples through their resources. Let's explore what we can and do some wondering together.

First mentioned is Mary Magdalene, who appears elsewhere in the gospels. We will explore her more fully in the next volume, but for now notice the description of her; she has had seven demons cast out. We have no idea what kind of demons are being referred to here, but we know that the word "demon" was used to describe many things that today we might categorize as minor illnesses. A demon could be a headache, or it could be epilepsy, much as the generic term "skin disease" might be psoriasis, chicken pox, or a temporary rash or case of acne. The use of the number seven, a potent number in the Hebrew tradition, is intriguing. Because God created the world in seven days, the number seven came to stand for perfection, or completion. Thus, Mary may well have had seven demons (ailments), or she may have had "a lot." Whether taken literally or symbolically the use of the word "seven" suggests a large number.

The other thing we need to know about Mary Magdalene is that she was not a prostitute, and the Bible never even implies it. The idea that she was a prostitute stems from a misguided sermon

51

BIBLE STUDY

New Testament Women
VOLUME 1
FOR
Progressive
Christians

offered in 594 by Pope Gregory the Great in which he referred to her as a "cheap and wanton" woman. What inspired him to say this is lost to history, but it has damaged her reputation ever since, which may have been Gregory's intent since we know that in the early church some people treated Mary Magdalene with more reverence than many men thought she deserved, and there were often efforts to paint her in a less-than-favourable light. In modern times, the production of _Jesus Christ Superstar_ in 1970 did not help Mary's cause. The line "and I've had so many men before" in the song "I Don't Know How to Love Him" strongly suggested that she was, at best, a woman who slept around, and Mary was tarnished for another generation. At best, all of this is a pity; at worst it's a clear example of the tendency of many to paint women in an appalling light. It confirms the sexism wherein it is acceptable for men to "sow their wild oats" while women are expected to remain pure and chaste.

What the New Testament _actually_ tells us is that Mary Magdalene stuck by Jesus when many others abandoned him, that she was present for the crucifixion _and_ for the resurrection (the only woman mentioned in all four gospels as being present on Easter morning), and that she was – according to John – the first person Jesus sent out to proclaim his resurrection, making her not only an apostle but a pretty important one at that.

Here, at the beginning of Luke 8, we are told that she and several other women funded Jesus' ministry, although the biblical text does not tell us how Mary got the money in the first place. The notion that it was earned through prostitution is not borne out anywhere in the text and tends to be a charge levelled only against Mary, not the other women, thus perpetuating the smear job that had been done on her.

For her part, we are told that Joanna is the wife of Herod's servant Chuza.[9] We know that Chuza was steward to Herod Antipas who ruled from around 4 BCE (upon the death of his father, King Herod) until 39 CE. He was thus ruler of Galilee at the time of the death of Jesus and was also the ruler who ordered the death of John the baptizer. He was thus not considered a kind man, to put

Jesus chose women as traveling companions, disciples, and patrons of his mission.
– Lucy Peppiatt, *Rediscovering Scripture's Vision for Women*

it mildly. It is interesting, then, that the wife of one of his top servants would go to Jesus for healing and would use some of her wealth (presumably her husband's wealth) to support Jesus.

Joanna is also present with Mary Magdalene and "other women" who go to the tomb on Easter morning. This could suggest that she and Mary Magdalene were close friends, not only during their time of supporting the ministry of Jesus, but afterwards. Given what we know about Chuza (or at least about his employer, Herod) we can probably assume that he would not have been much in favour of Joanna's decision to follow Jesus, and thus deduce that she left him. She would have been able to take a dowry or inheritance with her, and perhaps that is the money she used to support Jesus' ministry.[10] Such may also have been the case with Susanna, although we know nothing of her except her name. Of course, that any of the women are named is profound testimony to their significance, or to Luke's desire to point out their significance. Perhaps they were better-known, or their gifts were more important, or their family backgrounds warranted a mention.

Luke 8:1–3 mentions that there were "many others" as well. In their book *Social-Science Commentary on the Bible*, Bruce Malina and Richard Rohrbaugh note that it would have been quite unusual for any married women to travel with Jesus and his band of male followers. However, it would *not* have been unheard of if they felt they needed to repay Jesus for the healing each of them had received. They also may have been widows, in which case they would have been free from other family obligations and able to travel more freely. While this might well have been the case some of the "many others" and maybe for Mary Magdalene – whose name derives from the town she came from, Magdala, rather than that of a husband or father – it would not have been the case for Joanna who was married to Chuza, or perhaps divorced as we noted.

The unnamed women are interesting because we learn here that several women (at the very least five or six) supported the ministry of Jesus and were also presumably followers. Some believe the fact that most of them are not named is an indication that Luke did not hold them in much regard. However, women in general were seldom remembered and so by the time Luke was writing the gospel quite possibly most of the names had simply been lost. Conversely it may have been to protect their identity, though this seems unlikely, again because Luke was writing years after the events.

We've already noted that the women mentioned in Luke 8 have been healed of various "evil spirits and infirmities." We cannot know what these illnesses were, but we do know that many ailments rendered one ritually unclean and likely to be ostracized from involvement in community life. Jesus was known to heal such people and this potentially enabled them to return to fuller status, to be restored to community. However, if the rest of the community rejected the healing, didn't believe it or acknowledge it, it stands to reason that these people – women in this case – would want to stay in the Jesus community. This especially makes sense in Luke's gospel, where the boundaries of the community are continually being pushed wider, to welcome and include those whom society had rejected.

It's also possible that these women did not become followers of Jesus but still supported him from a distance. To support Jesus' ministry would have netted them respect and honour from the Jesus movement, which may have been something sadly lacking in their lives otherwise.

The verb used to describe the actions of the women is the same one used for Peter's mother-in-law: *diakoneo*. This could imply financial support, but it could also mean that they provided places for them to stay on their travels, or perhaps homes where the early Christian church could gather for worship. Author Richard Pervo has suggested that episcopal leadership (bishops) arose in the church to counter the power of wealthy benefactors. Given that the bulk of bishops were male, he suggests that this happened precisely to lessen the influence of these women.[11]

The bottom line is that Luke wants us to know that some significant, wealthy, and thus presumably influential women supported the Jesus movement and may have been an integral part of it. Their gifts and financial support were vital to the movement's

BIBLE STUDY

**New
Testament
Women**
VOLUME 1
FOR
Progressive
Christians

success. Beyond that, the fact that they came into their ministry after having been healed invites us to wonder how people might be similarly invited into community and ministry today.

The emerging Christian community

A subsequent study guide will look more closely at several women named in the book of Acts, but for now let's look at a single verse at the beginning of Acts that seems to describe what one could consider the first meeting of the church after Jesus' departure or "ascension." Acts 1:14 says, "All these were constantly devoting themselves to prayer, together with certain women, including Mary the mother of Jesus, as well as his brothers." "All these" refers to the 11 remaining core disciples after Judas suffered a rather gory death (Acts 1:18).

The only woman mentioned by name is Mary, the mother of Jesus, but there are "other women," and that is significant. As the community gathered to try to make sense of Jesus' death and resurrection appearances, to figure out what to do next and how to carry on the work of Jesus, women were included. For those who suggest that the early church was an entirely male operation, this is a blunt challenge. Women appear at various points in Acts – and are frequently mentioned in Paul's letters – so we can only assume that their role was similar to that of the men. To the extent that the women were able, depending on personal circumstances, they were involved in every aspect of the life of the early church.

During the life of Jesus, women were grateful recipients of his healing and teaching; and they were disciples, ones who followed Jesus and supported his ministry in a variety of ways. After his death, they continued their discipleship in equally myriad ways, including as apostles sent out to proclaim the good news. To suggest that they were anything less or to try and diminish their role is to deny the evidence presented to us.

Questions

■ Who do you think of when you hear the word "disciple"? How about "apostle"?

■ Why do you think Matthew points out the presence of women and children in the stories of Jesus feeding the crowds?

■ What do you imagine Peter's wife might have been like?

■ Why do you think she's not mentioned while her mother is?

■ Why might three of the gospels tell this short story about Jesus healing Peter's mother-in-law?

■ Why might some translations render the feminine version of "deacon" as "deacon's wives" rather than "female deacons"?

■ Luke tells us of "many" women who supported Jesus and his ministry with their resources. What might these women have been like?

■ Why might they have supported this ministry?

■ Joanna is described as the "wife of Herod's steward Chuza." What do you think of someone in such a position supporting Jesus? What risks might she have faced?

■ What might have caused church leaders to paint Mary Magdalene in a negative light?

■ What roles do you think women may have held in the early church?

■ What role might Mary Magdalene have played?

Mary and Martha

As we've seen, there were many women disciples. There were also a number of women who, although we have not met them in this study yet, stood up to Jesus, who challenged some of his beliefs and practices. Some women did both. Mary and Martha, two sisters from Bethany, have two brief but very significant encounters with Jesus, and Mary goes on to have a third encounter. In each instance, the women engage with Jesus about his teaching and, in the process of doing so, challenge the wider community to explore how the new Jesus movement welcomed women in ways that had not been seen before.

Luke 10:38-42

[38]Now as they went on their way, he entered a certain village, where a woman named Martha welcomed him into her home. [39]She had a sister named Mary, who sat at the Lord's feet and listened to what he was saying. [40]But Martha was distracted by her many tasks; so she came to him and asked, "Lord, do you not care that my sister has left me to do all the work by myself? Tell her then to help me." [41]But the Lord answered her, "Martha, Martha, you are worried and distracted by many things; [42]there is need of only one thing. Mary has chosen the better part, which will not be taken away from her.

While this brief story appears only in Luke's gospel, it has had a far-reaching effect on the Christian church. There are even people who are not Christian who know of the story, or at least know that there were two sisters and that one of them, Martha, seemingly got reprimanded for asking Jesus to discipline her sister. It's a curious story, to be sure, and it harbours a major textual problem that makes it even more interesting.

Verses 41 and 42 appear in a wide variety of forms in the ancient manuscripts, suggesting that early writers and editors fiddled with the verse in the earliest years. Why? We can only assume that they struggled with the verses in whatever version they found them and sought to improve upon them. Unfortunately, all of this makes it harder to know what the intent of the original writer might have been.

In one traditional understanding of the story, Jesus and the disciples have arrived at the home of Mary and Martha. Let's pause and notice this. Normally, a home would be identified in terms of the male occupant, but here it is referred to as "Martha's" home. It's also noteworthy that Jesus and the disciples don't raise their eyebrows at this, which perhaps means it *wasn't* noteworthy to *them*. They would have known there was no man present but do not seem to care. A household headed by a woman? No big issue.

While Jesus is teaching, Martha busies herself making sure they receive proper hospitality – that is, that a meal (possibly lavish) is prepared, so that they might be impressed in addition to being well-fed. Either way, lavish or not, preparing a meal for 13 men, including Jesus, plus themselves (so a minimum of 15 people total) would have been a lot of work. Martha notices that Mary is sitting at Jesus' feet *not* helping. Why on earth is she doing that, when she can readily see that her poor sister is working herself silly? Martha then confronts Jesus: "Don't you care that my sister has left me to do all the work myself?" And now it gets murky.

The *New Revised Standard Version*, while being literally accurate, leaves things ambiguous. What is Martha really worried about? Some translations, using one of the other versions of the Greek manuscripts, stretch it out a little to try to clarify Martha's complaint. J. B. Phillips rendered verses 41 and 42 this way: "But the Lord answered her, 'Martha, my dear, you are worried and bothered about providing so many things. Only a few things are really needed, perhaps only one. Mary has chosen the best part and you must not tear it away from her!'" In this way, Phillips suggests that Jesus says to Martha something more along the lines of, "You know, Martha, we don't need a six-course meal. Just a few dishes – or even just one – would be more than enough. Why don't you come and sit here for a while yourself, and then we can all make a stew together?" I know, that's not what the passage really says, but I believe it's close to where it may well have been going.

There is yet another way of looking at this, however, and it has to do with the ways in which we have traditionally translated the passage; this is the textual problem referred to above. Translating the Greek literally, the first part of verse 40 says, "But Martha was distracted (*or* pulled away) by *many serving tasks*," or (and this is where it gets really interesting) "*by much ministry.*" The word translated as "serving tasks" is *diakonia*, which is generally translated in terms of ministry whenever it refers to something men are doing – yet not so with women, and not so here. Why not? What is it we seek to hang on to traditionally that prevents us from believing a woman, in this case Martha, would be involved in ministry? After all, we see many times in the gospels that there was a great commitment to equality within the Jesus community. It stands to reason, therefore, that this could be a case of Martha being overwhelmed by the ministry she provides – cooking enough food for every meal to have lots left to serve the poor or visiting those who are poor and in need – that she is exhausted. When she sees Mary "just sitting there," something snaps for her, and she turns to Jesus for support.

Jesus, however, does not want to get into an argument between the two sisters and wants to affirm the choices both have made. Serving food and showing hospitality are vital and constitute ministry. Listening to Jesus is also vital and is ministry, too. Perhaps there are ways both can be affirmed. Dorothy Lee, in *The Ministry of Women in the New Testament*, points out that "the choice lies not between service and listening to the word, but rather between labouring with elaborate forms of hospitality and paying heed to Jesus' teaching."[12]

The issue that Martha seems to want to raise – and certainly what many biblical interpreters have sought to extract from this story over the years – is the proverbial tension between a contemplative life and a life of service. When I was in seminary it was often voiced as the distinction between being "pastoral" (that is, caring for one's flock) and being "prophetic" (that is, standing up for justice in the community). The contrast is frankly false – both are necessary – but it quickly became an important distraction for eager seminarians. Whom do we serve: those who pay the bills, or those who may be suffering more from unjust systems? We all knew that challenging unjust systems would ruffle feathers amongst the flock, and they were the ones who would pay our salaries.

It was a surprise, then, to hear a professor say to some of us rather quietly, "Why can't you do both? Why can't you see that both are vital parts of the ministry of following Jesus?" The professor was right, of course. There are times when one kind of ministry is needed, and times when a different kind is needed. The important thing is to notice that both are acceptable – and necessary – forms of following Jesus.

Martha knew how important hospitality is and believed she must do it to the utmost, as a way of showing that Jesus and his entourage were distinguished guests worthy of great service. Also, Martha knew that welcoming anyone who came to your door was a hallowed commandment and practice of ancient Judaism. While it may have been ignored by many over the centuries, this gospel re-emphasizes its importance in this story of Jesus' visit to Mary and Martha.

At the same time, Mary did something rather bold and outrageous: she sat squarely at the feet of Jesus, the one who is treated as a revered rabbi in this story. Normally women busied themselves preparing food while the men sat and discussed the issues of the day and put the world to rights. But Mary has chosen to be a part of that, and Jesus has not asked her to leave. This is crucial.

Martha, of course, does not understand what her sister is doing. Really, Mary, don't you know that women don't do that? Don't you know that your place is not in there, listening to the men, but in here, helping me? But Mary has heard Jesus proclaim enough times that there is a distinct equality between men and women,

---

New Testament Women
VOLUME 1
FOR
Progressive Christians

WESTERN WALL STILL DESPERATE

The Sons of Mary seldom bother, for they have inherited that good part;
But the Sons of Martha favour their Mother of the careful soul and troubled heart.
And because she lost her temper once, and because she was rude to the Lord her Guest,
Her Sons must wait upon Mary's Sons, world without end, reprieve, or rest.
– Rudyard Kipling, *The Sons of Martha*

BIBLE STUDY

New Testament Women
VOLUME 1
FOR
Progressive Christians

and thus that it is acceptable for a woman to listen to his teachings and, in good rabbinic fashion, to debate them with Jesus and the others. This will not be taken from her, Jesus declares. The implication could be that, by telling Martha that they really only need one dish of food, Jesus is offering a quiet invitation to her to join them and suggesting that perhaps all of them – men and women alike – can work together to prepare some food afterward. It would have been a radical idea at the time – but Jesus is all about radical ideas.

Some see in this story a larger piece as well – a statement about the roles of women and men in the early church. The fact that the third gospel refers to it as Martha's home immediately tells us that there is no male present, and thus that the older of the sisters (Martha) is in charge. House churches, the earliest form of Christian community after the death of Jesus, would have been organized by the head of the household, and thus Martha appears to be leading a house church. In the earliest days, churches split the duties of members between those who served and those who learned and studied and preached. Those who served presided over the sharing of food in a communal meal, pausing to remember Jesus' last supper with his disciples. These people would also have been in charge of making sure that the leftovers were distributed to those who were poor, to widows and orphans, and to those who were too sick to attend.

Over the years, the positions shifted somewhat in favour of those who took on the ministry of learning, studying, preaching. It became the sole property of this class to preach and to preside at communion, which is what the communal meal evolved into. As this position was elevated, the other was denigrated.

Does Martha symbolize this first ministry – that of overseeing the preparation of food, and presiding at the meal, and making sure the leftovers were distributed fairly? And does Mary represent those who spent their time debating the history of their people, and of God's connection to them, and Jesus' new approach to how to live as people of faith?

Is this story being used by each side to promote their viewpoint? This would certainly help explain the many ways the story exists in the ancient texts; people didn't fiddle with texts unless they disagreed with the point being made in the copy they had (whether it was original or not). There would undoubtedly have been those who wanted to elevate ministries of service (the Marthas) and those who wanted to elevate ministries of contemplation (the Marys). Interestingly, neither stance forces one to promote women over men, or vice verse. Perhaps Jesus is seeking to affirm that all jobs within the church can be held by whoever wishes to hold them, and whoever is trained or empowered to hold them.

John 11:1–6, 17–39

John 11 features two sisters named Mary and Martha, who will also feature in chapter 12. Are they the same women as in Luke? Tradition, and the fact that the names are the same, would suggest that they are. However, there are notable differences between Luke and John's portrayal of them. John does not report the spat between the sisters over work, and Luke does not tell us anything about the raising of Lazarus or that it was Mary who anointed Jesus.

Beyond that, there are three other factors that bring into question whether they are the same women. First, both names were very common in those days; just think of the number of women named Mary in the gospels and you realize that it would not have been unusual for multiple families to have both a Mary and a Martha. Second, Lazarus appears in John but is absolutely *not* present in Luke. Remember too that in Luke Jesus visits "Martha's home," which strongly suggests there was no man living there. Lastly, we have to consider that "facts" are secondary to the author of John – what is far more important is to make a lasting point, and if you have to fiddle with the facts a little so be it. Granted, "facts" may not have been top of mind for the author of Luke either – the birth narrative, after all, is most likely a work of fiction – but symbolism is clearly more important for the author of John than it is for the writer of Luke. The classic example of this is that John has Jesus crucified *not* on Good Friday, as the other gospels tell us, but on *Thursday* so that the crucifixion coincides with the

BIBLE STUDY

**New
Testament
Women**
VOLUME 1
FOR
Progressive
Christians

time that the Passover lambs were slaughtered. Powerful symbolism, but probably not at all factual. All of this is to say that John may well have constructed the story of the raising of Lazarus simply to portray Jesus' power.

This story is generally known as the raising of Lazarus, and that is clearly the focus for the writer. However, in order to keep *our* focus on the interactions and involvement of the women in the story, I have stopped the quotation just short of the miraculous resurrection or resuscitation.

John sets up the story so that Jesus will demonstrate the glory of God, and certainly raising someone from the dead would do that. It begins with a reference telling us that Mary was the one who anointed Jesus with perfume, except this story will not be told in John's gospel until chapter 12 – that is, *after* this current

John 11:1-6, 17-39

Now a certain man was ill, Lazarus of Bethany, the village of Mary and her sister Martha. [7]Mary was the one who anointed the Lord with perfume and wiped his feet with her hair; her brother Lazarus was ill. [3]So the sisters sent a message to Jesus, "Lord, he whom you love is ill." [4]But when Jesus heard it, he said, "This illness does not lead to death; rather it is for God's glory, so that the Son of God may be glorified through it." [5]Accordingly, though Jesus loved Martha and her sister and Lazarus, [6]after having heard that Lazarus was ill, he stayed two days longer in the place where he was.

[17]When Jesus arrived, he found that Lazarus had already been in the tomb four days. [18]Now Bethany was near Jerusalem, some two miles away, [19]and many of the Jews had come to Martha and Mary to console them about their brother. [20]When Martha heard that Jesus was coming, she went and met him, while Mary stayed at home. [21]Martha said to Jesus, "Lord, if you had been here, my brother would not have died. [22]But even now I know that God will give you whatever you ask of him." [23]Jesus said to her, "Your brother will rise again." [24]Martha said to him, "I know that he will rise again in the resurrection on the last day." [25]Jesus said to her, "I am the resurrection and the life. Those who believe in me, even though they die, will live, [26]and everyone who lives and believes in me will never die. Do you believe

one. This may simply reflect sloppy editing; John might have originally placed the other story first, and then it got moved (such things
really do happen by accident in all sorts of manuscripts).

John next tells us that Jesus loved Mary, Martha, and Lazarus,
yet Jesus decides to wait rather than go to see them when he first
hears that Lazarus is ill. It's as if Jesus wants Lazarus to die – or at
least to get sicker – so that the miracle he performs will be that
much more powerful. In verse 14, Jesus tells the disciples that
Lazarus has died, and then suggests they head off to see him. As
Jesus approaches Bethany, Martha hears of it and goes to meet
him, saying (rather caustically, one imagines), "You know, if you'd
been here my brother would not have died. Yet I'm sure you can
do something." When Jesus says that Lazarus will rise again, Martha
offers the tepid, "Well, yeah, I know he'll rise on the resurrection

BIBLE STUDY

**New
Testament
Women**
VOLUME 1
FOR
Progressive
Christians

this?" [27]She said to him, "Yes, Lord, I believe that you are the Messiah,
the Son of God, the one coming into the world."

[28]When she had said this, she went back and called her sister Mary,
and told her privately, "The Teacher is here and is calling for you."
[29]And when she heard it, she got up quickly and went to him. [30]Now
Jesus had not yet come to the village, but was still at the place where
Martha had met him. [31]The Jews who were with her in the house,
consoling her, saw Mary get up quickly and go out. They followed her
because they thought that she was going to the tomb to weep there.
[32]When Mary came where Jesus was and saw him, she knelt at his feet
and said to him, "Lord, if you had been here, my brother would not
have died." [33]When Jesus saw her weeping, and the Jews who came
with her also weeping, he was greatly disturbed in spirit and deeply
moved. [34]He said, "Where have you laid him?" They said to him,
"Lord, come and see." [35]Jesus began to weep. [36]So the Jews said, "See
how he loved him!" [37]But some of them said, "Could not he who
opened the eyes of the blind man have kept this man from dying?"
[38]Then Jesus, again greatly disturbed, came to the tomb. It was a cave,
and a stone was lying against it. [39]Jesus said, "Take away the stone."
Martha, the sister of the dead man, said to him, "Lord, already there is
a stench because he has been dead four days."

day." Jesus then offers what seems to be the real point of the story: "I am the resurrection and the life."

What happens next sometimes gets lost in the emphasis on Lazarus and his death, but it is an astonishing moment: Martha says, "I believe you are the Messiah." This is the first such proclamation in John's gospel, although Peter comes close in John 6:69 where, after Jesus explains about the need to eat his flesh and drink his blood, Peter exclaims "You have the words of eternal life. We believe and know that you are the Holy One of God." Some later versions of the Greek manuscript add the statement "you are the Christ" presumably to make this more consistent with Matthew 16:16, where Peter makes a similar confession, and to take the emphasis away from Martha.

Yet it is far more likely that in John's gospel Martha's bold proclamation in 11:27 is the first such statement of faith, making it highly significant. If this Martha is indeed the same woman as in Luke 10, then her ministry seems to involve far more than serving food and providing hospitality; she seems to be a rather astute preacher, too.

Following this, Martha leaves and gets her sister Mary, who rushes out and kneels at Jesus' feet. Again, if these are the same women as in Luke 10 it is intriguing that in Luke she sits at his feet, here she worships at them, and in chapter 12 she will anoint them. Mary then makes the same statement that her sister made – that if Jesus had been there her brother would not have died.

Jesus prepares to raise Lazarus from death and, just as he does so Martha cautions him – you don't really want to have the rock removed from the mouth of the cave; the stench is going to be awful! It's a practical statement and shows us a caring side on the part of Martha. She would love to have her brother back, but at what cost?

Theologians tend to focus entirely at this point on the raising of Lazarus, on how Martha does not really believe ("Don't do it; he'll stink," she says), and on the contrast between how Lazarus comes (bound) but Jesus did not in *his* resurrection – an "observation" that is extremely hard to defend because the gospels stories make no claim one way or the other about what happened at the precise moment of Christ's resurrection. For our purposes, though, the significant piece has come earlier – the declaration by Jesus that he is the resurrection and the life, and Martha's recognition of who Jesus is. Considering that John will present another woman (Mary Magdalene) as the first to witness and believe in the risen Christ, and then to proclaim to others that Christ was risen, it appears that John wants to make a point about women here. They are not merely decorative. They are not confined to the kitchen, and they are not afterthoughts. Rather, they are front and centre in the dramatic events of the life of Jesus, and they are proud proclaimers of truths that have permeated the ages.

John 12:1–8

The final appearance of Mary and Martha comes closely on the heels of the previous story.

John 12:1–8

Six days before the Passover Jesus came to Bethany, the home of Lazarus, whom he had raised from the dead. [2]There they gave a dinner for him. Martha served, and Lazarus was one of those at the table with him. [3]Mary took a pound of costly perfume made of pure nard, anointed Jesus' feet, and wiped them with her hair. The house was filled with the fragrance of the perfume. [4]But Judas Iscariot, one of his disciples (the one who was about to betray him), said, [5]"Why was this perfume not sold for three hundred denarii and the money given to the poor?" [6](He said this not because he cared about the poor, but because he was a thief; he kept the common purse and used to steal what was put into it.) [7]Jesus said, "Leave her alone. She bought it so that she might keep it for the day of my burial. [8]You always have the poor with you, but you do not always have me."

While Jesus is at the dinner table with several others, and Martha served the meal, Mary comes in with a pound of pure nard and anoints Jesus' feet and wipes them with her hair. It is an extremely intimate moment. It is also fraught with wonderings related to the other gospels.

According to Luke 7:36–38, an unnamed woman anointed Jesus' feet with ointment and wiped them with her hair at the home of Simon, a Pharisee. John 12:1–8 closely parallels this story except that the element of forgiveness crucial to Luke is lacking here. That, in turn, makes John seem a little closer to Mark 14:1–11 (and its parallel in Matthew 26:1–16) concerning an unnamed woman who anoints Jesus' head at the home of Simon (a leper) in Bethany. The bottom line seems to be that John may have known both previous stories – either from their respective gospels or from other sources – and has somewhat combined them.

The cost of the perfume is exorbitant – over 300 denarii, which translates roughly to a year's wages. That's expensive perfume, no matter how you slice it. It was also imported, for nard came primarily from the Himalayas, which is a long way from Palestine. In other words, John is surely exaggerating, presumably to make the point that Mary wants to demonstrate a completely over-the-top amount of love and loyalty to Jesus.

Judas comments that buying the perfume was a waste of money and, to be honest, I want to agree with him. Don't you think Jesus would have agreed with him, too, perhaps thanking Mary but wishing the money had been used to alleviate hunger and suffering? Instead, in the story Jesus notes that she has prepared it for the day of his burial. Except that Jesus is still alive, and will be for another week, give or take.

If we remember that John prefers to use symbolism to get his points across. Mary is undoubtedly overwhelmed with gratitude because Jesus has recently brought her brother back to life, and so no gift would be too extravagant from that perspective. This alone is a powerful lesson for us: when faced with what God has done, the only reasonable response is overwhelming gratitude, the kind Mary showed. The church has variously used this story to point out how much devotion we should offer to Jesus, and that we will always have the poor with us. Yet presumably those who heard Jesus offer this part of a familiar teaching and law knew what it said in its entirety: "Since there will never cease to be some in need on the earth, I therefore command you, 'Open your hand to the poor and needy in your land'" (Deuteronomy 15:11). In other words, the poor will always be with us, so give what you can to them – always. This is contrasted with Judas who, we are told, was a thief who used to dip his hand into the coffers of the movement for personal benefit.

All that said, the point of the story seems to be open to interpretation. Is it simply to show how important Jesus is? Is John reminding us that the end is near? Is he recognizing Mary for (symbolically, at least) proclaiming Jesus' worth and value to the world?

According to John, Mary wipes Jesus' feet in the same way that Jesus himself will soon wipe the feet of the disciples, clearly modelling servant leadership in a most blatant way. In both instances the point may well be simply to notice that one cannot stop the world from turning the way it does, and the things of the world from happening – or as Lynn Japinga says it, "to stop the political and religious machine from rolling on and destroying" Jesus[13] – but we can still serve one another, we can still honour and affirm one another. This is a powerful teaching that Jesus shares by washing the disciples' feet; Mary shows us the same thing. Added to Martha's proclamation that Jesus is the Messiah, and the proclamation of Mary Magdalene that Jesus is risen, John shows us truly amazing examples of ministry.

Questions
■ What have you heard about Mary and Martha?
■ Have you been led to prefer one to the other?
■ How do you hear Martha's complaint about her sister?
■ How do you understand Jesus' response?
■ How can we reconcile different aspects or expectations of ministry?

BIBLE STUDY

**New
Testament
Women**
VOLUME 1
FOR
Progressive
Christians

■ How has your denomination understood definitions of ministry, especially when it comes to male versus female?

■ What do you make of Martha and Mary's confrontational statements to Jesus ("if you had been here my brother would not have died")?

■ What do think of the idea that greater emphasis was put on the raising of Lazarus over the years in order to diminish Martha's bold proclamation that Jesus was the Messiah?

■ Why might John report Martha's statement but not Peter's from earlier?

Women Set Free

The gospels include a number of stories about women who were set free from various ailments. These are more than just healing stories, however, for they contain an element that goes beyond simple physical healing to include liberation – liberation from an ailment and toward a fuller life. Given that in biblical times people generally assumed that anyone with an illness or ailment must have done something to displease God, the liberation involved is often to new life or restored life within the community. Let's look at these stories individually noting their similarities and differences and exploring how they depict Jesus giving life and wholeness.

The first one to look at is the story of the hemorrhaging woman, which comes in the middle of the second story we shall look at. While there is some connection between them, it helps to look at them separately first.

Mark 5:24b–34

And a large crowd followed him and pressed in on him. [25]Now there was a woman who had been suffering from hemorrhages for twelve years. [26]She had endured much under many physicians, and had spent all that she had; and she was no better, but rather grew worse. [27]She had heard about Jesus, and came up behind him in the crowd and touched his cloak, [28]for she said, "If I but touch his clothes, I will be made well." [29]Immediately her hemorrhage stopped; and she felt in her body that she was healed of her disease. [30]Immediately aware that power had gone forth from him, Jesus turned about in the crowd and said, "Who touched my clothes?" [31]And his disciples said to him, "You see the crowd pressing in on you; how can you say, 'Who touched me?'" [32]He looked all around to see who had done it. [33]But the woman, knowing what had happened to her, came in fear and trembling, fell down before him, and told him the whole truth. [34]He said to her, "Daughter, your faith has made you well; go in peace, and be healed of your disease."

BIBLE STUDY

**New
Testament
Women**
VOLUME 1
FOR
Progressive
Christians

The male oppression of women is not a women's problem. It is a man's problem ... men have to come to terms with.
– Chung Hyun Kyung, *Struggle to Be the Sun Again*

This woman has been bleeding vaginally for 12 years. That's a long, long time. Beyond that, it made her ritually unclean – perpetually. While this was only a public issue if she wanted to attend the temple, she also could not marry, for sex with a bleeding woman was forbidden. She is thus very much alone and has lost all her money spending it on doctors for no benefit. Presumably, when all this began, she would have been wealthy, as only the elite in society could afford the ongoing services of a physician, so she has also suffered the humiliation of having lost her standing in society. She may also have lost a marriage, although we are not told so.

The bottom line here is that her communal life, her life with others, is effectively over and has been for 12 long years. It's worth noticing that number for a brief moment for it was seen as a number of wholeness: there were 12 tribes in Israel, and so 12 was often seen as number of completion or fullness. This does not mean that the woman was not in fact bleeding for all that time, but those hearing the story might have twigged to the fact that she has been unclean for a perfectly long time.

Lynn Japinga points out that there were rules for menstruating women, generally presumed to have been put in place by men who found it "sinful, disgusting, and shameful." Yet Japinga goes on to point out something else: "It is possible that the rules existed not so much because menstruation was gross and disgusting but because it was mysterious and powerful ... The ability to bleed and not die was particularly strange, in a 'wow, that's amazing' way more than an 'ooh, that's disgusting' way."[14]

Recently a news item on television reported that the government of British Columbia was going to make menstrual care products available for free in all the province's schools. Someone made a comment about how this might seem unfair to men. A woman quickly piped up, "Hey, we can't help it if we bleed." There was a small public outcry over what some saw as an overly bold statement by a TV reporter, but many quickly came to her defence. Why do we have difficulty mentioning something as natural and healthy as women bleeding? What is it about menstruation that still, in the 21st century, challenges our (or at least male) sensibilities?

Regardless of the reasoning behind this biblical law, the woman undoubtedly knew that it was risky to interact directly with Jesus – simply touching his body or his clothing would have rendered him unclean, and for any woman to speak to a man in public would have broken cultural taboos. She decides, instead, just to try to touch the edge of his robe. This action could be attributable to a primitive sense of magic, the belief that somehow there would be a mysterious healing property invested in the clothing of a holy man like Jesus, but the woman seems to put more emphasis on Jesus' personhood. He is the one with whom she would like to have contact, but she does not dare.

BIBLE STUDY
**New
Testament
Women**
VOLUME 1
FOR
Progressive
Christians

Interestingly, Mark goes into far more detail in this story than do either Matthew or Luke, who strip the story down to its bare bones. Luke does not include the woman's inner conversation about touching the hem of Jesus' robe, and neither of those gospels contain Jesus' immediate awareness that something has happened, that some mysterious "power" had gone out of him.

Some have suggested that this story was shortened because while it was too well known in the early Christian community to be ignored, the topic itself was a bit difficult and uncomfortable. Mark, however, wants us to know that Jesus immediately sensed someone had touched him, with purpose.

The disciples are incredulous, thinking "Oh come on – there's a huge crowd here! You really think one person's touch was different than another's?" But Jesus knows, somehow, that someone has touched him with a desire to be made whole, to be healed, to be set free. And he looks around to see who it was.

The woman then approaches Jesus in "fear and trembling" believing that she has done something terribly wrong and is about to be called out for it. She must have been stunned, then, when Jesus called her "Daughter." This is not a patronizing term, but recognizes her not as "some nameless, bleeding, unclean woman in the crowd" but as a daughter of God, a child of the covenant; in other words, as nothing less than a person. Jesus has restored her to full humanity. Or, as Lynn Japinga puts it, "Touching Jesus healed her body. Talking to Jesus healed her soul."[15]

Jesus says, "your faith has made you well" or "has saved you," which has more of a sense of overall well-being.[16] Many have sought to see this story as Mark's rejection of Levitical purity laws, but Mark doesn't mention that at all. On the other hand, the woman has spent all "her" money suggesting she was independently wealthy. She does not slip away quietly when confronted with what she has done, but rather boldly – if with a fearful heartbeat – comes forward and says, "It was me." In response to this, Jesus affirms her.

Mark 5:22-24, 35-43

[22]Then one of the leaders of the synagogue named Jairus came and, when he saw him, fell at his feet [23]and begged him repeatedly, "My little daughter is at the point of death. Come and lay your hands on her, so that she may be made well, and live." [24]So he went with him.

And a large crowd followed him and pressed in on him... [story of the woman with the hemorrhage].

[35]While he was still speaking, some people came from the leader's house to say, "Your daughter is dead. Why trouble the teacher any further?" [36]But overhearing [or ignoring] what they said, Jesus said to the leader of the synagogue, "Do not fear, only believe." [37]He allowed no one to follow him except Peter, James, and John, the brother of James. [38]When they came to the house of the leader of the synagogue, he saw a commotion, people weeping and wailing loudly. [39]When he had entered, he said to them, "Why do you make a commotion and weep? The child is not dead but sleeping." [40]And they laughed at him. Then he put them all outside, and took the child's father and mother and those who were with him, and went in where the child was. [41]He took her by the hand and said to her, "Talitha cum," which means, "Little girl, get up!" [42]And immediately the girl got up and began to walk about (she was twelve years of age). At this they were overcome with amazement. [43]He strictly ordered them that no one should know this, and told them to give her something to eat.

This story of the healing/resurrection of a young girl frames the story about the bleeding woman. They share a few similarities in that each concerns a female (a woman and a young girl) with an ailment, who encounters Jesus and is healed. Neither female is named at the outset, and yet both are given "names" by Jesus: the woman is called "Daughter" and the child *"Talitha"* or "Little Girl." Granted, those are hardly proper names, but in contrast to the oblivion of namelessness they carry a certain weight, for in naming the women Jesus affirms their personhood. Also, the child is 12 years old, and the woman has been bleeding for 12 years, suggesting that Mark might have intended to draw a link between the two.

Jesus learns of the little girl's illness via her father, a devout man who, like the woman, falls at Jesus' feet. According to Mark, Jesus goes with Jairus but enroute encounters the woman and interacts with her. In Matthew's gospel, the little girl has already died; in both Mark and Luke, however, she is initially reported as being very sick, to the point of death. It is only after the encounter with the woman that word comes to say that the child has died. And here arises a textual problem.

The narrator says the girl is dead and clearly the people believe it as mourners have begun to gather. Yet Jesus says she is asleep. It seems we always assume the girl is in fact dead; it is tradition. But the account contradicts itself: some people think the girls is dead, and Jesus says she is not. Who are we to believe? It's a curious thing. It seems we want to portray Jesus as so powerful he can raise a dead person, and so his own statement simply gets in the way of a miracle.

What if Jesus is *not* mistaken? What if the little girl is, in fact, not dead but only sleeping or even comatose? We should not see this as diminishing the miracle; it's still amazing that he restores her to health. One also wonders if there is something else at play here. Perhaps the father's concern is that the daughter has just reached marriageable age, and her death could cause major problems in terms of cancelling an inter-family alignment. But Jesus goes into the house and sends everyone else out. He speaks to the girl and she gets up and walks. Jesus' response? He tells her family to get her something

BIBLE STUDY

**New
Testament
Women**
VOLUME 1
FOR
Progressive
Christians

to eat. In other words, treat her like the living, breathing human being that she is. As Jesus did with the woman who was bleeding, he does again now: he proclaims publicly that someone who was written off deserves more than that. That makes this a bigger story about the worth and value of women and children.

John 7:53 — 8:11

[[[53]Then each of them went home, 8[1]while Jesus went to the Mount of Olives. [2]Early in the morning he came again to the temple. All the people came to him and he sat down and began to teach them. [3]The scribes and the Pharisees brought a woman who had been caught in adultery; and making her stand before all of them, [4]they said to him, "Teacher, this woman was caught in the very act of committing adultery. [5]Now in the law Moses commanded us to stone such women. Now what do you say?" [6]They said this to test him, so that they might have some charge to bring against him. Jesus bent down and wrote with his finger on the ground. [7]When they kept on questioning him, he straightened up and said to them, "Let anyone among you who is without sin be the first to throw a stone at her." [8]And once again he bent down and wrote on the ground. [9]When they heard it, they went away, one by one, beginning with the elders; and Jesus was left alone with the woman standing before him. [10]Jesus straightened up and said to her, "Woman, where are they? Has no one condemned you?" [11]She said, "No one, sir." And Jesus said, "Neither do I condemn you. Go your way, and from now on do not sin again."]]

This is how the *New Revised Standard Version* presents the text of this story. The double brackets have been inserted by the editors of this version to indicate that scholars generally agree that this story was not originally part of the gospel of John, since many of the ancient manuscripts do not include it at all. Other manuscripts include it with the equivalent of an asterisk, suggesting it was suspect even in ancient times. Still other manuscripts include it after John 7:36, or after John 21:25 (at the very end of the gospel), or even after Luke 21:38. Clearly people have been unsure of the status of this story from the beginning. In any event, while it might be a true story, at the very least it's doubtful that it comes from the same hand that wrote the rest of John's gospel.

BIBLE STUDY

New Testament Women
VOLUME 1
FOR
Progressive
Christians

All that said, it's a great story. While on the surface it is a story about a woman, it is also much more. As Jaime Clark-Soles points out in *Women in the Bible*, "if this woman 'caught in adultery' is caught in anything, it's a male pissing contest."[17]

Some men bring to Jesus a woman who has been "caught in the very act of committing adultery." The first question we must ask is, "If she was caught in the very act of committing adultery, where is the man with whom she was committing this act?" Of course, he's long gone. To quote Clark-Soles again, "Laws governing sexuality are typically applied more severely to women than to men."[18] Immediately they seem to be showing their own incompetence either by not catching the man, or by their failure to recognize/acknowledge that such an act involves a minimum of two people.

They make the woman stand before Jesus and state their case, asking Jesus what they should do. The Law of Moses, they claim, says she should be stoned, which is not quite true; it states that both she *and* the other party should be stoned. Beyond that, they would have known that Roman law did not permit such a punishment; are they simply challenging Jesus to defy the Roman law so they can turn him in?

Jesus stands up; most English Bibles say he "straightened up" but the Greek verb is the same here as the one in verse 3, which is translated "stand up." Thus, he faces those who are making the accusation and he meets the woman face to face, perhaps making eye contact in a way that is affirming and expresses to her that everything is going to be okay. He then silently draws or writes

BIBLE STUDY

New Testament Women
VOLUME 1
FOR
Progressive Christians

The truly wise person kneels at the feet of all creatures and is not afraid to endure the mockery of others.
– Mechthild of Magdeburg

something in the dirt. When they keep questioning him, Jesus stands up again and says, "Whoever has never done anything wrong should throw the first stone," and goes back to drawing in the dirt. When he stands up again, they've all left. Facing the woman as an equal, Jesus tells her to go and sin no longer.

We tend to interpret that last bit as Jesus making his judgment on the woman. But that is based on the assumption that "sin" means "wrongdoing." Yet sin is more often understood as a state of being, specifically the state of being separated or cut off from God. Jesus does not condemn her for anything she has done. It's sort of like when one is pulled over for speeding and the police office gives you a warning rather than a ticket. You were in fact speeding but are let off the hook. Is that what Jesus is saying? If so, he certainly downgrades the "evil" of being caught in adultery.

Perhaps this is really a story about hypocrisy, a story about people condemning someone else when they will not acknowledge their own mistakes. Beyond that, it is a powerful story that suggests men and women should be treated fairly, and most impor-

Janet Jackson

During the halftime show of the Super Bowl football game in 2004, one of the performers, Justin Timberlake, tore at the bodice of the costume she was wearing, accidentally or otherwise exposing her breast for roughly one half second.

The aftermath was fascinating, if also appalling and stunning. Timberlake was allowed to participate in the Grammy Awards the following week, but Jackson had her appearance cancelled by the show. She experienced several other cancellations, while Timberlake was generally left unscathed.

Stop and notice for a moment that Jackson did nothing wrong other than be a woman who, by nature of her gender, had breasts. Timberlake was the one who exposed her breast, yet she was the one who was punished.

Clearly some ancient stories still come to life today.

tantly, *equally*. If the men have been "let off the hook" so to speak, so should the woman be. It's worth noting what Jesus dares to do when it would have been so much easier just to go along with the good old boys. Instead, he puts her on a level playing field with the men accusing her and essentially invites us to judge them all the same. Finally, Jesus may also recognize the possibility that the woman was no willing participant in the act being committed; she may very well have been assaulted or forced into sex against her will. This was a common occurrence in those days, especially considering the country was occupied by a foreign army. Thus, condemning her would have been a double wrong since the Law of Moses forbade forced sex.

Whether this story was originally part of the gospel or not is almost irrelevant at this point. The story has been offered to us from the earliest of times, undoubtedly because it shows Jesus standing up to a group of men in defence of a vulnerable woman.

B I B L E S T U D Y

**New
Testament
Women**
VOLUME 1
FOR
Progressive
Christians

Luke 13:10-17

[10]Now [Jesus] was teaching in one of the synagogues on the sabbath. [11]And just then there appeared a woman with a spirit that had crippled her for eighteen years. She was bent over and was quite unable to stand up straight. [12]When Jesus saw her, he called her over and said, "Woman, you are set free from your ailment." [13]When he laid his hands on her, immediately she stood up straight and began praising God. [14]But the leader of the synagogue, indignant because Jesus had cured on the sabbath, kept saying to the crowd, "There are six days on which work ought to be done; come on those days and be cured, and not on the sabbath day." [15]But the Lord answered him and said, "You hypocrites! Does not each of you on the sabbath untie his ox or his donkey from the manger, and lead it away to give it water? [16]And ought not this woman, a daughter of Abraham whom Satan bound for eighteen long years, be set free from this bondage on the sabbath day?" [17]When he said this, all his opponents were put to shame; and the entire crowd was rejoicing at all the wonderful things that he was doing.

BIBLE STUDY

**New
Testament
Women**
VOLUME 1
FOR
Progressive
Christians

This story of Jesus healing – on the sabbath, no less – a woman who is bent overis unique to Luke. It has several intriguing elements via which Jesus (and/or the author of Luke) pushes the boundaries of what is acceptable in society versus what is acceptable to God. In the end, the latter seems to win through hands down.

Several years ago, I attended the ordination of Anita Hill to ministry in the Evangelical Lutheran Church in America (ELCA). Anita was a lesbian in a committed relationship, and the ELCA forbade the ordination of non-celibate members of the LGBTQ+ community. However, her congregation wanted her ordained and decided to bring in Bishop Krister Stendahl – a renowned theologian and respected church leader from Sweden – to ordain her. At the point in the service where the bishop was to ask if there were any objections, Stendahl put his head down so that even if someone had raised a hand he could not see it. He then lifted his head and said, "I see no opposition, so she shall be ordained." While largely symbolic, it was a powerful way for Stendahl to say that those who wished to oppose God's will in this ordination were not worth seeing, and not worth acknowledging.

Jesus does the opposite with the woman who is bent over, choosing to see her when others would not. Both Jesus and Stendahl, through their select vision, chose to make bold statements about who is included in the people of God. Our decision about who we see can be life-giving.

Jesus is teaching in a synagogue on the sabbath. He notices a woman who has been crippled for 18 years and is thus unable to stand up straight. We do not know why she is so inflicted. Is it physical? Has she been beaten? Or is it psychological? Has she been called names and put down so often that she feels she is worthless? Have poverty or other social ailments caused her to be bent over? Whatever the cause, the infliction has been long lasting and debilitating.

The gospel first tells us it is the result of a spirit, and later (verse 16) Jesus says she has been "bound by satan." We need to remember that "satan" is not a proper name in the New Testament, but rather is the title for anyone who is diametrically opposed to God; it refers to a person or persons who take a stand that is in conflict with God. Those forces can be almost anything, but it is intriguing that they are seen as being what has crippled this woman, suggesting that it is indeed the specific acts of others that have rendered her unable to stand with dignity.[19]

Jesus sees her, lays hands on her, and declares her healed. Immediately, she stands up straight and praises God. The leader of the synagogue (male, of course) is furious, saying in essence, "This is the sabbath! She's been crippled for 18 years; surely she could have waited one more day to be healed." But Jesus' approach is entirely different. He challenges the leadership, saying, "Why should she wait one more day? Indeed, one more minute? You guys would lead a donkey to water, yet you think I should not save a woman's life and dignity? Boy, are you twisted."

We are *not* called to defend rules that conflict with giving life and wholeness to others. If helping another person requires breaking the law, break it. If helping another person requires going against scripture, do it. If anything conflicts with helping another person feel noticed, loved, or affirmed, do whatever you can to help them feel noticed, loved, and affirmed.

No wonder Jesus' opponents are put to shame and the crowd rejoiced. We have to wonder, of course, if the synagogue authorities would have objected so strongly if Jesus had healed a man.

In any event, Jesus points out that the woman is nothing less than a daughter of Abraham and Sarah. In other words, she is a child of the covenant and thus a child of God who deserves better treatment than the men want to offer her. Jesus offers healing; the men choose to argue about it. Yet Jesus will not back down; he is adamant that "mercy and healing [are] more important than keeping a rule."[20]

This story, like the others we have looked at in this session, reminds us of the importance of noticing and "lifting up" others, especially those who are *not* being noticed or supported by those in

BIBLE STUDY

**New
Testament
Women**
VOLUME 1
FOR
Progressive
Christians

authority. We are called to recognize people's worth and dignity simply because they are human; no other requirement is necessary.

Questions

■ The woman with a flow of blood who approaches Jesus seems to risk everything in order to receive the healing she believes he can offer. What do you think of her approach? How much would you risk?

■ In the story of Jairus' daughter, those who claim to take the Bible literally tend to fixate on how Jesus resuscitates a dead child. Yet Jesus says she is only sleeping. Do you believe him? If not, why not?

■ The story of the woman caught in adultery may not have originally been part of the gospel. What impact does learning this have on the value of the story for you?

■ What is this story about for you?

■ What point(s) do you see Jesus making?

■ Reflecting on the story of Anita Hill and Krister Stendahl, what other instances of people noticing – or not noticing – others to make a point can you recall?

■ What do you think of the story of Jesus healing the woman who is bent over?

■ Why do you think she was bent over?

■ The Pharisees make a valid point. After all, she has waited 18 years for healing; can't she wait one more day? Yet Jesus challenges this idea. What are your thoughts?

■ In what situations have you felt called to go against the law or scripture?

1. Jane Schaberg, "Luke," in Carol A. Newsom and Sharon H. Ringe, eds., *The Women's Bible Commentary* (Louisville: Westminster/John Knox Press, 1992), 275–292.

2. Bruce J. Malina and Richard L. Rohrbaugh, *Social-Science Commentary on the Synoptic Gospels* (Minneapolis: Augsburg Fortress, 1992), 261.

3. Robert McAfee Brown, *Unexpected News: Reading the Bible with Third World Eyes* (Louisville: Westminster John Knox Press, 1984).

4. Raymond E. Brown, *The Birth of the Messiah,* rev. ed. (New York: Doubleday, 1993), 299.

5. https://en.wikipedia.org/wiki/Saint_Anne

6. Dennis E. Smith and Michael E. Williams, eds., *The Storyteller's Companion to the Bible: John* (Nashville: Abingdon, 1996), 42.

7. Mary Ann Getty-Sullivan, *Women in the New Testament* (Collegeville, MN: The Liturgical Press, 2001), 223.

8. Malina and Rohrbaugh, *Social-Science Commentary*, 181.

9. Ibid., 334.

10. "Jezebel 2" in *Women in Scripture: A Dictionary of Named and Unnamed Women in the Hebrew Bible, the Apocryphal/Deuterocanonical Books, and the New Testament,* Carol Myers, ed., (Boston: Houghton Mifflin, 2000), 213.

11. Richard Pervo, "Unnamed Women Who Provide for the Jesus Movement" in *Women in Scripture*, 885.

12. Dorothy A. Lee, *The Ministry of Women in the New Testament* (Grand Rapids: Baker, 2021), 52.

13. Lynn Japinga, *From Daughters to Disciples: Women's Stories from the New Testament* (Louisville: Westminster John Knox Press, 2021), 79.

14. Ibid., 26.

15. Ibid., 27.

BIBLE STUDY

**New
Testament
Women**
VOLUME 1
FOR
Progressive
Christians

16. Amy-Jill Levine, "Woman with a Twelve-Year Hemorrhage," in *Women in Scripture*, 849–850.

17. Jaime Clark-Soles, *Women in the Bible: Interpretation: Resources for the Use of Scripture in the Church* (Louisville: Westminster John Knox, 2020), 203.

18. Ibid., 204.

19. Getty-Sullivan, *Women in the New Testament*, 83.

20. Japinga, *Daughters to Disciples*, 33.

BIBLIOGRAPHY

Brown, Raymond E. *The Birth of the Messiah.* rev. ed. New York: Doubleday, 1993.

—. *The Gospel According to John.* Garden City, NY: Doubleday, 1966.

Brown, Robert McAfee. *Unexpected News: Reading the Bible with Third World Eyes.* Louisville: Westminster John Knox Press, 1984.

Clark-Soles, Jaime. *Women in the Bible: Interpretation: Resources for the Use of Scripture in the Church.* Louisville: Westminster John Knox Press, 2020.

Gafney, Wilda. *A Women's Lectionary for the Whole Church: Year W.* New York: Church Publishing, 2021.

Getty-Sullivan, Mary Ann. *Women in the New Testament.* Collegeville, MN: The Liturgical Press, 2001.

Japinga, Lynn. *From Daughters to Disciples: Women's Stories from the New Testament.* Louisville: Westminster John Knox Press, 2021.

Lee, Dorothy. *The Ministry of Women in the New Testament.* Grand Rapids: Baker, 2021.

Malina, Bruce J. and Richard L. Rohrbaugh. *Social-Science Commentary on the Synoptic Gospels.* Minneapolis: Augsburg Fortress, 1992.

Meyers, Carol, ed. *Women in Scripture: A Dictionary of Named and Unnamed Women in the Hebrew Bible, the Apocryphal/Deuterocanonical Books, and the New Testament.* Boston: Houghton Mifflin, 2000.

Newsom, Carol A. and Sharon H. Ringe, eds. *The Women's Bible Commentary.* Louisville: Westminster John Knox Press, 1992.

Smith, Dennis E. and Michael E. Williams, eds. *The Storyteller's Companion to the Bible: John.* Nashville: Abingdon, 1996.

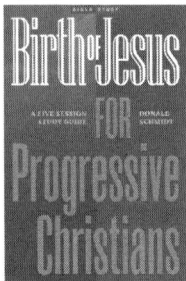

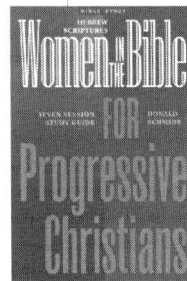

THE POWER OF STORYTELLING IN WORSHIP AND EDUCATION
A Practical Guide

Jed Griswold

A resource for pastors, religious educators, teachers, and parents.

Think about how Jesus taught. And rabbis. How have Buddhist monks taught children and adults for centuries? How have Hindu swamis taught? And Islamic leaders? And Indigenous elders in lands around the globe?

It is difficult to overstate the importance of storytelling when it comes to our desire to pass along our values, our spirituality, our faith to the next generation. Or to teach and inspire our own generation.

In this small book you will find perhaps the most concise and well-articulated guide to storytelling anywhere. Jed Griswold's 12 tips for storytelling and his 20 original stories are more than enough to clarify and inspire readers to engage in the art of storytelling. It also includes a sample lesson plan, which is available as a free download.

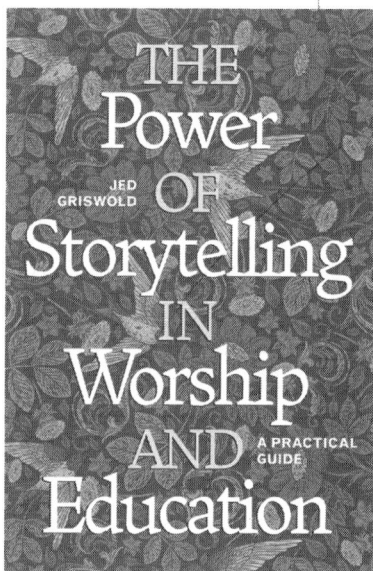

ISBN 978-1-77343-519-0 | 112 pages | 4.75" x 7" | $14.95

HOW THE LIGHT SHINES
Stories, Strategies, and Spiritual Practices for Caregivers of People with Dementia

Trisha Elliott

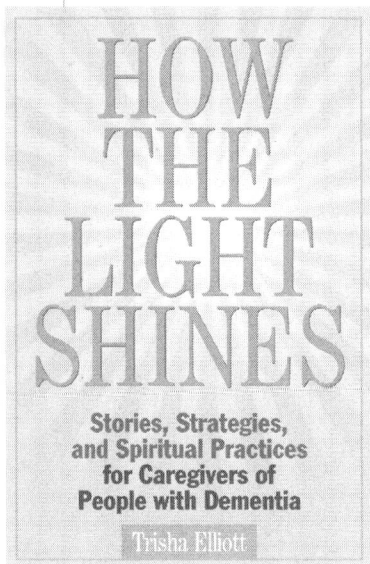

This book is for caregivers who have a desire not only to hone their caring skills, but also to deepen their relationship with God through their care. It explores feelings of loss and challenge, but turns always towards potential and hope. There are over 100 types of dementia affecting over 50 million people around the world. Unfortunately, knowing the hard numbers doesn't make caregiving less demanding, challenging, exhausting, and yet in many ways, potentially uplifting. Caregiving is typically understood as an activity, as something we do – likely because caregivers do a lot. But caregiving is deeper than what we do. It is more than a series of tasks. It is, first and foremost, a call to love.

Regular Edition: ISBN 978-1-77343-526-8 | 176 pages
6" x 9" | $24.95
Pocket Edition: ISBN 978-1-77343-285-4 | 176 pages
4.75" x 7" | $19.95

ALPHABET OF FAITH
26 Words about Faith, Ethics, and Spirituality

Sara Jewell

Weaving together faith and culture, this breathtaking book explores what it means to live a life of faith and spirit in the 21st century. It brings together 26 "words" – such as energy, justice, liminal space, and X marks the spot – that reflect the challenges and joys of living in our beautiful but broken and often brutal world.

It is unwaveringly contemporary, progressive, and thought-provoking. The pieces are written for those who say they are spiritual but not religious, for people who are or may be familiar with church but perhaps don't attend anymore, for those who know Jesus and his teachings and are familiar with the Bible, even if they haven't opened it in awhile.

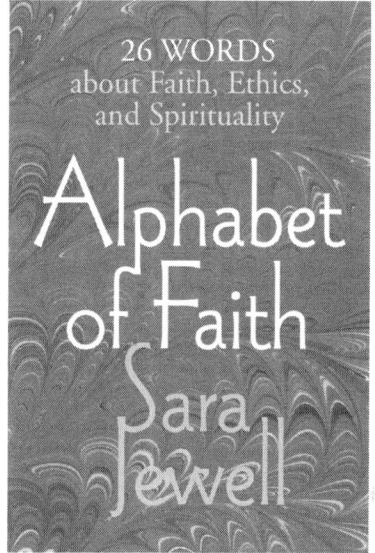

ISBN 978-1-77343-517-6 | 256 pages | 4.75" x 7" | $24.95

WOOD LAKE
Imagining, living, and telling the faith story.

WOOD LAKE IS THE FAITH STORY COMPANY.

It has told
- the story of the seasons of the earth, the people of God, and the place and purpose of faith in the world;
- the story of the faith journey, from birth to death;
- the story of Jesus and the churches that carry his message.

Wood Lake has been telling stories for more than 35 years. During that time, it has given form and substance to the words, songs, pictures, and ideas of hundreds of storytellers.

Those stories have taken a multitude of forms – parables, poems, drawings, prayers, epiphanies, songs, books, paintings, hymns, curricula – all driven by a common mission of serving those on the faith journey.

Wood Lake Publishing Inc.
485 Beaver Lake Road
Kelowna, BC, Canada V4V 1S5
250.766.2778

www.woodlake.com